DARE TO LEAD

Timothy Foster

D1397588

A Division of G/L Publications
Glendale, California, U.S.A.

Scripture quotations are from the *New American Standard Bible.* ©The Lockman Foundation, 1971. Used by permission.

Second Printing, 1977

Published by REGAL Books Family Life Division
G/L Publications
Glendale, California 91209
Printed in U.S.A.

Library of Congress Catalog Card No. 76-57013
ISBN 0-8307-0519-8

I wish to express appreciation
to my wife Donna,
and our daughters Tanya and Tara,
for their diligent support,
patience and encouragement in this project.
My thanks also to James Killion
of Dallas Seminary
for his thoughtful editorial help,
and to my secretary Nancy Shirk,
for her faithful assistance.

CONTENTS

*A study guide for individual or group study
is available for this book.*

FOREWORD

Becoming a father takes no great skill or special ability; being a father is, unfortunately, quite the opposite. While this dilemma is generally recognized, not much has been done to solve it. Society, Christians included, is saying a great deal about sex, but dreadfully little about being a dad.

If you're standing in a bookstore pondering the wisdom of investment in this little book, or at home in your favorite chair wondering what your wife wants you to read now, take heart. *Dare to Lead* is worth your investment—be it time, money or both. Dr. Timothy Foster knows his stuff. I've read this book (twice), and I know his children (well). So if the commendation of a sometimes frustrated father means anything to you, read on, brother!

Tim and Donna Foster were married the same day Kathi and I were—they in Florida, we in California—August 10, 1968. Eight years later we were driving the Pennsylvania Turnpike together, going to bicentennial Philadelphia to celebrate our anniversaries. As we drove —without the two girls each couple had produced—we talked about *Dare to Lead*. Tim was frustrated. Should he continue writing about fatherhood or spend his evenings at home being a husband and father? The problem was not new to him—or to anyone in vocational ministry. Do you tell others what God has shown you, or do you show your family?

Later, as we walked toward the Philadelphia waterfront, we stopped to read a plaque marking the site of Dr. Benjamin Rush's home. Tim related that Rush, a signer of the Declaration of Independence, was not only active in the colonial cause, but, as a physician, was the father of psychiatry in America. Furthermore, Rush was a Christian—a believer whose knowledge of God dominated his outlook on life. In short, Rush was a be-er, a doer, and a teller—a man free to serve others.

We walked on and went into Bookbinders for lunch, and like countless tourists before us, swooned over their bouillabaisse. The conversation eventually returned to the question: Do I write or do I be?

I'm not sure now how that discussion ended—or even if that was the last time we pondered it together.

Obviously, Tim finished the book. But now that I've read the book, the question has been answered. The answer is found in the two reasons I'm recommending this book to you: one, what Tim has to say is biblical (and accordingly practical and helpful); and two, I realize now that Tim's question did not have an "either-or" answer. His book and life have answered it eloquently as a "both-and." Tim not only says it in *Dare to Lead*, he lives it with his wife and two girls. Like Benjamin Rush, Tim is a be-er, a doer, and a teller—a man free to serve others.

Jim Killion
Dallas, Texas

PREFACE

This book is written for men. If you feel your wife bought this book to "straighten you out," you may not want to read about how to be the leader in your home. You may even be feeling a bit resentful. If so, I suggest that you read just chapter 1 and *then* decide about reading the rest of the book.

Frankly, I put off writing this book several times. I felt as though my own marriage and family relationships should be such that I would be worthy of writing a book about them. I have given up on that. So I am not saying "Here's how to be as good a leader in the home as I am." Rather, I am sharing some ideas based on biblical principles which have been valuable to me as husband, father and head of my house.

I have tried to make the book as concise as possible so that you can pick it up and read it quickly. My hope is that you will even feel like rereading it in six months or a year.

PART I

PRINCIPLES OF LEADERSHIP
IN THE HOME

1
STANDING IN LINE WITH THE KING OF THE CASTLE

One of my favorite stories is about two gates in heaven. Over one gate is a large sign which reads, "All men who have been dominated by their wives, stand here." Standing at that gate is a line of several hundred men. Over the other gate is a sign which says, "Men who have never been dominated by their wives, stand here." At that gate stands one man, looking somewhat bewildered.

Seeing the man, Saint Peter walks over and says, "Why are you here?"

"I don't know," he replies, "my wife told me to stand here."

Contemporary Kings and Queens
Whether we admit it or not, most of us have been

affected at one time or another by uncomfortable feelings of being dominated. If we choose not to be dominated but rather to be leaders in our own homes, then how do we lead our families?

Many of our wives are far better educated than their mothers. Many have skills and professions that have little or nothing to do with being a wife or mother. Women are now realizing they don't need us in order to survive. Those still depending on us are being pressured to change their ways and establish their own identity.

We've heard some men wistfully longing to go back to the days when they could keep their women illiterate, barefoot and pregnant. Those days are gone forever.

Some fathers of generations past seemed to be successful at being the leaders in their homes. Unfortunately, most of them didn't tell us how to do it. Even if they did, or if we imitated what we remember seeing them do, we could be using methods that would not work at all with today's women.

We have a difficult time finding someone to use as a model. Television and movies provide more negative than positive models. They often portray a man as stupid and totally controlled by his wife, his children or his sexual impulses. On the other hand, even while giving us poor models, our culture has given us unrealistic romantic expectations that are contradictory to the way things really are. Perhaps the easiest way to identify our own expectations is by checking our mental images.

King of the Castle Image

When you read the phrase "head of the house," what mental image do you get? Take a minute to look at the first mental picture your own mind gives you of "The Head of the House."

Here's one mental picture:

It's Saturday afternoon. A man is sitting in his reclining chair with his feet up. He's watching a football game on the TV in front of him. On the man's left is a bowl of pretzels. On his right, a tall glass of Pepsi with plenty of ice. The head of the house is barking out orders like a sea captain, and his family is rushing to obey.

"Cathy, I'm out of Pepsi."

"Susie, daddy needs some more pretzels."

"Philip, the football field needs to be a little more green, and those jerseys are blue, not purple."

There he sits, enthroned, the head of the house!

Although details of our mental pictures were different, most of us probably had some variation on the theme that "head of the house means being king of the castle." In the pages to come, we will examine a biblical model for leadership and compare it to these "king of the castle" expectations.

In the first part of the book we will sketch a perspective for the husband—a biblical and practical perspective—which is vital to the structuring of our roles as heads of our houses.

In the second part of the book we will discuss the major issues we face as the heads of our houses—issues like what to do when our wives are upset, directing our children toward healthy concepts of their sexuality, setting boundaries for good discipline, how to end an argument, how we affect our children's relationship to God, and other matters that we can learn to handle skillfully and thus provide more effective leadership for our families.

2
THE MODEL SERVANT

When it comes to Bible verses about the marriage relationship, the three-to-one favorite of men everywhere is "Wives, be subject to your own husbands, as to the Lord" (Eph. 5:22). That verse fits into our "king of the castle" expectations just fine, doesn't it? One of you fellows just made a note reminding yourself to make your wife call you "Lord" from now on. But not so fast. We get into an inaccurate perspective when we read only the verses intended for others.

Look at the verse again. It's addressed to wives. We seem to have little problem in telling wives to submit, while we ignore the biblical admonitions to husbands.

Recently a man named Dan was in my office with his wife. "What do I do when my wife just won't obey God's Word and obey me like the Bible says?" he asked.

"What's the problem," I asked, "can you be specific?"

"She won't mow the lawn, even though I tell her to," he replied.

"Tell me about that," I asked his wife Jan, beginning already to have some idea about the family situation.

"I did do it for most of the summer, but he has me driving a school bus in the morning and afternoon and selling Tupperware at night. Plus I have two preschool children and he insists I keep the house perfectly clean. I don't see why he can't mow it," she challenged.

"You know very well that I work all day and when I come home at night I'm tired," he countered.

In front of me was a man who had very definite ideas about what his wife should do, and a Bible verse (he thought) to *make* her do it, but he regrettably didn't have any idea of his own responsibility toward his wife.

Since this book is written for men, we'll not make further reference to how our wives ought to submit. Now that I've quoted the standard verse about wifely submission and you know that I know that it's in the Bible, we can accomplish a lot more by reading the verses addressed to us.

The Principle of Servanthood

The Bible has several important verses recognizing the man as "head" in marriage and telling men how to lead as Christ led. The key verses are Ephesians 5:23 and 25,

> For the husband is the head of the wife, as Christ also is the head of the church . . . . Husbands, love your wives, just as Christ also loved the church and gave Himself up for her.

These verses not only tell us to love our wives, they also tell us to love them like Christ did and to give ourselves up for them.

The next thing we need to do is find out what our

model, Jesus Christ, meant by giving Himself up for the Church. Our minds go first to Christ's giving up His life for our sins, but that's probably the least directly applicable part of the model. Probably none of us will be required literally to die so that our wives can live. Even if we were willing, we won't really be given the opportunity. There is more to the model than sacrificing our own lives as Christ did.

Let us turn first to Philippians 2:3-8:

> Do nothing from selfishness or empty conceit, but with humility of mind let each of you regard one another as more important than himself. Look out for the interest of others and not just for your own personal interests. In other words, have the same attitude in yourselves which was also in Christ Jesus, who eternally existing in the same essence as God, did not regard equality with God, in form, a thing which He must maintain. So He emptied Himself, taking the form of a love-servant, and being made in the likeness of men, ... He humbled Himself (author's paraphrase).

How well does our husband example Dan measure up to the principle of servanthood described in these verses? If we arrange these verses from Philippians into a True/False check list, we can determine if Dan's behavior was exemplary.

Check True or False for each description as it applies to Dan.

True False
1. ☐ ☐ Selfishness
2. ☐ ☐ Empty conceit
3. ☐ ☐ Humility

4. ☐ ☐ Regarding the other as more important
5. ☐ ☐ Looking out for his own personal interests
6. ☐ ☐ Looking out for the interests of others
7. ☐ ☐ Having a Christlike attitude
8. ☐ ☐ Maintaining a position of superiority
9. ☐ ☐ Emptying himself
10. ☐ ☐ Taking on the form of a love-servant

The Christ Model

Our model in Ephesians 5:23 and 25 can be summarized like this: "Husbands are to their wives as Christ is to the Church." Most of us like the sound of that because it imparts a godlike quality to the position of husband. Further, the idea of being to our wives like Christ was to the Church usually brings the focus of attention to leadership.

On a plane one afternoon, I found myself chatting with a Mr. O'Conner. He saw I was working on this book and we talked a little about it being directed to husbands. After a few minutes of conversation, he surprised me by asking, "How can I make my wife respect me? Sometimes she laughs right in my face. Nothing makes me madder than having her ridicule me. I wish I could be a strong enough leader so that she wouldn't dare do that for fear of her miserable life."

Mr. O'Conner, frustrated and angered, admitted that he was a weak leader. He knew that he lacked his wife's respect and felt helpless to do anything about gaining it.

Maybe your wife is more like Ken's. Ken's wife didn't laugh at him, but she would often ask questions like, "Where do you think we should put the new chair?" When Ken gave her his opinion, she promptly put it where she had originally intended, totally ignoring his input.

At times when she felt there was a problem between their son and his wife, she would ask Ken, "What can we do about it?"

Ken would say, "Stay out of it. It's their life."

She usually reacted by saying something like, "Even if you don't care about our son's happiness I'm not going to sit by and watch them suffer if I can tell them how to avoid it."

When I asked Ken what kind of a leader he thought he was at home, he gave me a bitter smile and said, "Are you kidding? You've seen how she talks to me. She wouldn't follow me to the corner drugstore."

Dan and Ken have somewhat extreme situations with both their wives evidencing need of some major overhauling and tune-up. (Incidentally, Ken's wife also needs some body and fender work.) How did these men get to be in such circumstances, the one coming for marriage counseling and the other willing to ask help from a psychologist he had just met on an airplane? Both had problems of leadership and both dreamed of the day when they could say "jump" and their wives would ask "how high?" They wanted to be strong leaders who commanded respect.

The Servant Leader

If then we are to lead like Christ led the Church, it would be appropriate to study what He has to say about leadership.

Christ explains how He sees His leadership of the Church in the parallel passages of Matthew 20 and Luke 22. The context of Matthew 20 is that the mother of the sons of Zebedee has come to Jesus asking for leadership places in His kingdom for her sons. (To digress for a moment, an interesting story is implied here. Where was Zebedee? Why is the boys' mother speaking for them?

If Zebedee had been the kind of leader he might have been, could this story have happened?)

Christ answers the question of Zebedee's wife by saying that she does not know for what she is asking. Further, He says that whoever wants to be great must be as a servant, just as He, the Son of man, came not to be served, but to serve.

The context of Luke 22 is that of the Last Supper and an argument among the apostles as to which of them was to be regarded as greatest.

In verses 25-27, Christ replies to this issue by saying, "The kings of the Gentiles lord it over them; and those who have authority over them are called 'Benefactors.' But not so with you, but let him who is the greatest among you become as the youngest, and the leader as the servant. For who is greater, the one who reclines at table, or the one who serves? Is it not the one who reclines at table? But I am among you as the one who serves."

Thus, the Son of man did not come to be served, but to serve, and to give His life a ransom for many. We have assumed that it is better to be served, but Christ said He came to be our leader by serving us.

Ephesians 5:1 tells us to be imitators of God. Jesus, as our godly model, made giving Himself up a way of life. He began by giving up His omnipresence in order to take on the limited form of a human body. He gave of His strength to heal and to help. He gave up His life to save us. Why did He do that? To meet our needs. We not only needed His ultimate giving of Himself to make payment for our sin, we also needed His life to show us the new way, to be our model. We find, then, that the core principle of Jesus' life and death is that of servant-hood.

Even as I write this I feel myself saying along with many readers, "Do you know how hard that is? Do you know what you're asking? Doesn't the head of the house have a right to be comfortable? Isn't that why the Lazy Boy recliner was invented?" The answer is that we are told to do as Christ did, and that is to put the comfort and convenience of our family above our own.

It was certainly more "comfortable" for Christ in His limitless, godly form than it was in His very limited form of a human. His priority was our need for a savior. The Garden of Gethsemane prayer makes it clear that Jesus would have preferred to do something other than suffer pain to meet our needs. He didn't die for us because it was fun. He died for us because we needed it. Already that sounds like we've got our work cut out for us. Jesus did whatever was necessary to meet our needs. He is our model.

Compare Christ's concept of leadership as portrayed in these verses to the image of the "head of the house" described watching football in the first chapter. That image saw a man expecting to be served because he was the head, the leader. But the biblical model of leadership is exactly opposite to the "serve me first, I'm the king of the castle" model. Christ said, "I am the one among you who does the serving." Not only does Jesus lead that way, but He clearly says that if we wish to lead in His kingdom, we must do the same.

The Servant-Leader Responsibility

Christ's style of leadership is further emphasized in John 13:12-15,

> And so when He had washed their feet, and taken His garments, and reclined at table again, He said to them, "Do you know what I have done to you? You call me Teacher, and

Lord; and you are right; for so I am. If I then,
the Lord and the Teacher, washed your feet,
you also ought to wash one another's feet. For
I gave you an example that you also should do
as I did to you."

This was the scene at the Last Supper in the Upper
Room: It was always the responsibility of the host to
provide a servant at the door to wash the feet of guests.
As the disciples had borrowed the use of the room, there
was no host. The disciples' need—the washing of their
dirty feet—was therefore unmet. By His servantlike actions Christ clearly told the disciples that they were to
take the responsibility to see to it that people's needs are
met, just as He did. In the future they were not to sit
around and assume these tasks were going to get done
for them because they were leaders. On the contrary,
because they were leaders, they needed to be the ones
doing the serving.

I can't speak for everyone here, but I know I have
trouble assuming that servant-leader role. Because my
wife is the wife and I am the head of the house, I have
often assumed that she will automatically take care of
certain tasks. As I look back, my assumptions were apparent when our children were small and not yet sleep-
ing through the night. I would usually just roll over and
go back to sleep, figuring that my wife would meet the
needs of the children. According to the verses in John
13, it would have been better if I had assumed the
responsibility and had at least shared it, rather than
assuming that my wife would serve.

Christ's servanthood is as much an Old Testament
concept as it is a New Testament concept. In passages
of Isaiah, the Messiah is prophesied in what have been
called four Servant Songs. Through the words of the
prophet, we see God calling His Son by a title. The title

is "My Servant" or the "Suffering Servant." We read, for instance, these phrases: "Behold, My Servant will prosper," "My Servant will justify the many."

Christ's servanthood was one of the reasons why the Jews did not accept Christ as the Messiah. They thought the Messiah, the leader-savior and the servant, would be two different people. They couldn't imagine any one person both leading and serving, but Christ was just that—both leader and servant—and we can be the same.

What Would You Do?
On the basis of Philippians 2:3-8, check True or False for each description as it applies to you in your own relationship with your wife in the last two weeks.

True False
1. ☐ ☐ Selfishness
2. ☐ ☐ Empty conceit
3. ☐ ☐ Humility
4. ☐ ☐ Regarding the other as more important
5. ☐ ☐ Looking out for one's own personal interests
6. ☐ ☐ Looking out for the interests of others
7. ☐ ☐ Having a Christlike attitude
8. ☐ ☐ Maintaining a position of superiority
9. ☐ ☐ Emptying yourself
10. ☐ ☐ Taking on the form of a servant

Evaluate by your responses whether you are moving strongly toward the biblical servant-leader model.

FOR FURTHER THOUGHT
Where Are You Now?
• Use the following Scripture and queries to guide you in assessing yourself as head of your home.

a. What differences do you see between your commitment of love and leadership to your wife and that described in Ephesians 5:23-25?
b. In what ways does your leadership in your home follow the servant-leader principles described in Philippians 2:3-8?

Where Do You Go from Here?
- Make a list of the changes you believe you need to make in your leadership to more closely follow Christ's servant-leader model.
- What are at least three decisions and actions you will take this week to help make these changes?

3
THE FREEDOM TO SERVE

Probing further into the servant/leader concept, we read in Galatians 5:13, ... "For you were called to freedom, brethren; only do not turn your freedom into an opportunity for the flesh, but through love serve one another."

An often-asked question is "If I'm head of my house, don't I have the freedom to do what I want?" This verse says we have freedom, but it does not say to use that freedom to serve our own desires. On the contrary, we have been given freedom so that we can minister or serve and meet the needs of our family.

Sometime ago I had a very unhappy wife and a short-sighted husband coming to see me about their problems. The wife and her husband worked full-time and both earned good wages. They told me they had several bank accounts between them. With the money she earned, she bought food for the three teenage children and her husband and herself. She also made house payments and paid many miscellaneous bills. With his money he paid some of the utilities (usually late) and made payments on his camper, his boat and his truck. He always had at least 100 dollars cash in his pocket, and his wife was not permitted to ask how he spent that or any of the rest of "his" money. He had gun collections, fishing rod collections, tape decks and all kinds of adult "toys" and hobbies.

His wife regularly pleaded for some of "his" money and he regularly got quite angry when she brought up the subject. It is interesting to note that he was a generous tipper. He left silver dollars wherever he went. Meanwhile, his family suffered.

This is an example of a man who saw himself as the king of his castle. He said the money he earned was for him. He used it to satisfy his own selfish desires. He was a big tipper in order to feel big himself. He said, "I am free to do whatever I want with it." He misused his freedom.

The Problem of Tyranny

Many who consider themselves strong leaders misuse their freedom and invite similar problems. Al was one of these. Things were fairly calm at home during the day. In the late afternoon, however, the atmosphere noticeably changed. The children became nervous. His wife became irritable. At 5:00 P.M. when he walked in the door, dinner was to be put on the table. Most of the family ate it in silence. Al preferred it that way. If anyone talked at dinner, it was almost always Al. No one was allowed to disagree with or discuss one of his snap decisions. Al wanted no back talk. Al talked, but Al never listened. His family was constantly afraid of him. Al was a Christian and a deacon, but Al was also a tyrant. He believed God wanted him to rule with an iron hand, and so he did just that.

The Bible, however, doesn't support Al's way of family living as being Christlike. God's Word tells us that as God's children we have not been given a spirit of fear, but Al's family was afraid. The problem that made Al a tyrant was his fear of any possible challenge to his authority. He arbitrarily decided to protect himself from any such possibility. He wanted only to meet his own needs.

Keeping the Balance

God condemns tyranny in our homes by Christ's instruction and His modeling of the use of authority only for the benefit of others.

Collectively, the Scriptures issue a well-defined directive to us in our roles as husband/leaders. *We have been given no authority to command anyone to do anything to meet our own needs.* I know that's hard to swallow. I don't blame you for blinking at that, but it is our cultural expectations that make us blink, not our theology. We've seen some of the key Scripture verses which link leadership to serving and meeting the needs of others. Can you think of any verses that give us authority for any other reason? I'm not talking about verses to our wives, remember, I'm talking about verses to us. A careful scrutiny of the Scriptures reveals that there are no verses in the Bible which give men authority over their families in anything except in meeting the needs of their families.

The Bible seems to be teaching that we cannot tell our wives to do something if it is for our own convenience only. We can surely ask them to do something for our convenience as they can ask us. But we cannot command or expect them to do things *for us* simply because we say so.

On the other hand, when you are meeting the needs of a member of your family or a need of the family as a whole, you can give very clear and direct instructions. Commanding your wife and children to salute you would be in bad taste, but you can give directions for their good.

My wife has a very definite dislike for dentists. She calls it hate. She is also cavity-prone. The two problems are probably connected in some way. Nevertheless, every few months or so, she will mention a toothache. If she can help it, she won't mention it until she's having to eat cream of wheat for dinner, but sooner or later the truth is out. In this case, my wife has a need. She needs to see a dentist. She needs my help in meeting that need because she won't go on her own initiative. When this happens it is both very important, and, in my opinion, necessary, for me to say to her, "I want you to call a dentist today and make an appointment as soon as possible. I will call you at noon, and if you haven't done it by then, I will do it for you."

Those are very strong and clear directions, but she rarely balks at them. That's because she knows I am doing it for her good and not for my own. (The only thing I get out of the directive is a dental bill.) I've discovered that when my wife is not cooperating with me, usually, it is because I am trying to meet my own needs, rather than hers or the family's.

The same is true with our children. "Go shine my shoes" is commanding them to a task the sole (no pun intended) purpose of which is to meet my own needs. I have no authority for such a command.

Who decides what the family's needs are? Who decides how to meet them? Who decides whether it is to meet their own needs or my own? The answer to all of these questions is you, the head of the house.

The Problem of Abdication

We mentioned tyranny earlier. The failure to look after the emotional, physical, intellectual, as well as spiritual needs of your wife and children, is to be guilty of the opposite of tyranny—abdication.

Abdication is nothing other than a refusal to lead. Many men who lead very competently at work, allow (or more accurately put, they cause by default) their wives to run things at home. This is not loving leadership. It is the refusal to accept God's call to be the head of the house.

If your wife is running things at home, rather than blaming her desire to wear the pants in the family, perhaps it would be better if you blamed this situation on your own fear or unwillingness to wear them. This unhappy circumstance is further complicated by the fact that once you have discovered your mistake and want to lead, it is very hard for wives, having once been the leader, to learn how to follow.

FOR FURTHER THOUGHT
Where Are You Now?
- How do you show your authority as leader of your home?
  a. In what ways have you been using your leadership to tyrannize?
  b. In what areas have you been abdicating your leadership?
  c. In what recent situations have you given absolute instructions to your wife or children when you

would have been wiser to give them freedom of choice?

d. In what instances have you given freedom of choice when you should have provided absolute instructions?

Where Do You Go from Here?

- List at least three specific areas or situations in which you need to provide clearer leadership. Rank these in order of importance to you and to your family.
- What can you do this week to strengthen the first area you have listed? The second area? The third area?

4
THE SUBMISSION QUESTION

A few months ago I was teaching a group of men in a week of meetings at a church. I had just presented the model of Christ as a servant-leader, when an older man (we'll call Mr. Martin) interrupted me somewhat angrily. His question went something like this: "You seem to be saying that husbands should be submissive to their wives instead of the other way around. Won't that get the whole family messed up?"

That's a difficult question to answer because there are so many implications in it. If a man places himself under the leadership of his wife, and trusts that whatever decision she makes will be the best, and believes that if she does make a mistake the responsibility is between her and God, then the answer to that man's question is yes. The family will get messed up.

Mr. Martin's question also says "if he is submissive instead of his wife." That implies she is not submissive. When the wife is in the driver's seat and the husband is along for the ride, she will end up a very frustrated woman.

I had a regular patient who placed himself under the leadership of his wife in this manner. His two favorite words were "Yes dear," and he said them quite often. He was unwilling or unable to stand up to her or to make a firm decision based on a conviction between himself and the Lord. His wife became an angry old lady and he became a mental patient. This family was, in Mr. Martin's vernacular, "messed up."

What if the husband is submissive to the wife's leadership and she is submissive to his? Certainly that condition sounds better than the first one, but if we look at it more carefully, it's not really right either. What we have here is abdication. Neither spouse is willing to stick his or her neck out and make a decision. Granted, it is more pleasant hearing two people say, "Whatever you want, dear." "No, dear, whatever you want will be just fine," than to hear "We'll do it my way or not at all." But when no one leads, how can two people walk together in the same direction? There is a lot more to being head of the house than just sounding sweet.

Spiritual Subjection

There is still another aspect to that gentleman's question that we have not yet discussed. Are men supposed to be subject to their wives? We can't just say, "No!" and move on. That would be giving a purely emotional response. Let's look at the facts.

We have initially defined subjection as placing oneself under the leadership or headship of someone who, therefore, assumes a certain responsibility. When I teach a course in marriage and the family, I usually talk to the girls about finding a guy who demonstrates that he can see her needs and meet them better than she can meet them herself. I tell them to look for a man they can trust to take care of them rather than a man they think they can change into something worthwhile. They are to look for a man they can happily follow.

These principles operated in reverse for a patient who talked to me about discontinuing his therapy. "I found a woman who can really take care of me," he said. This reverse in role was the attitude that his wife needed to have about him!

By scriptural definition and example, men are not to be in subjection to their wives. We will resist the temptation to talk about what our wives should do, and look at two verses of Scripture directed to us.

The first verse is Ephesians 5:21, which tells all of God's children to place themselves in subjection to one another in the fear or reverence of Christ. Does this verse include husbands? It would appear that it does.

It's important that we resolve this apparent conflict between everyone being in subjection in verse 21 and only wives being in subjection in verse 22. The resolution will give us another principle we need to apply to our leading as Christ did. I believe the answer is in a second definition of the word "subjection" which can also mean "giving priority or preference to someone else."

The qualifying phrases in Ephesians 5:21 and 5:22 help us understand these verses in light of these two definitions of the word "subjection."

In verse 22, wives are told to be in subjection to their husbands, with the qualifying phrase "as to the Lord." This implies leadership, responsibility and authority. Wives are to subject themselves to their husbands in the same way that all of God's children subject themselves to Christ.

The qualifying phrase in verse 21 is different. It says we are all to be subject to one another "in the fear of Christ." Here the second definition—giving priority or preference to others—seems to apply.

The implication of this qualifying phrase, within the context of this verse, could be that if we fear Christ, we will not consider those for whom He died to be of low value. Consistent with that is the fact that a reverential awe of Christ does more than anything else to create a sense of humility within the heart of man.

The verse telling us all to be in subjection to one another is telling us to be humble, to put others' needs as more important than our own. This is exactly consistent with the servant-leader concept.

Ephesians 5:21 is a parallel passage to Romans 12:10: "Be devoted to one another in brotherly love; give preference to one another in honor." The kind of subjection referred to in Ephesians 5:21 and in Romans 12:10 means that we are to respect our wives as being of high individual value and worth; at least as worthy as we are.

Leadership and Equality

Our discussion of spiritual subjection brings us to the important difference between leadership and equality and the importance of maintaining a delicate balance between them. The nature of our headship in the home is in function or role, not in worth. We have been given specific jobs to do in the family. Our wives have been given other jobs to do. Both of these roles are given. Nothing we have ever done as men has made us more deserving of leadership positions than our wives. The book of Ephesians was written, giving us that role, long before we were born. We did nothing to earn it.

I have always resented it when people who are taller than I am make reference to their height as though they had somehow achieved it by personal effort or had earned it in some way. That attitude of "I'm superior to you because I am taller" is just as much prejudice as saying, "God loves me more because I'm white and you're black." Many of us erroneously think that whatever traits we have are somehow better than whatever other people have.

We dislike this same attitude when we see school children making fun of a child with some birth defect, such as a malformed limb or deafness. The superiority of function that the whole children have is not something to brag about; this superiority is in function only, not in worth.

Applying this principle to our function as heads of our homes, we recognize first of all that we stand before God with our wives and children as individuals of equal value to Him. We are all equally and individually responsible before God and we are all equally unworthy of His love. God didn't make men the head of the house because He loved us more. He made us head of the house because He designed us to do that job, with His help. In other words, husbands and wives are all equally worthy, valuable and responsible to God, but we have different functions in our homes.

Overwhelming Leadership
One of the most common mistakes men make in trying to lead their families is to confuse these two issues of function and worth. When we do that, we tend to overwhelm the individuality of the other members of our household. One way we do this is by talking down to our wives, as though they were our children. This makes them feel squelched, put down, and resentful.

41

Just this morning I counseled with a patient, a lady in her fifties, who said, "My husband treats me as if I were his daughter. He tells me what to do and how to do it. He insists I fold his underwear the way his mother did. It's ridiculous. Unless I sneak off to the store by myself, he'll tell me everything from which cantaloupe to pick out to which pantyhose to buy. How can he possibly know more about pantyhose than I do? I must be awfully stupid." She was also very angry.

After hearing about this incident, one man I know was brave enough to ask his wife if she felt he ever talked down to her and if so, what specific phrases she disliked. After she recovered from the pleasant shock of his question, she said, "Yes, I guess there are one or two phrases that make me feel like a child." She frankly told him what these were. As he worked on avoiding these and treated his wife as an equal, she began to be a more confident adult.

To test yourself regarding this facet of overwhelming leadership, listen to yourself for phrases you might be using with your wife that are similar to words your parents used with you. Phrases like, "How many times do I have to tell you this?" and "When will you ever learn?" are examples. If you find you are using these phrases, you may have a problem with underestimating your wife. Even if you don't think you underestimate your wife, by using these phrases you sound to your wife as if you do underestimate her.

Try also to be aware of just thinking "parental" phrases about your wife. Even if you don't say them, the attitude is still there and your wife can easily detect it. On the other hand, when she feels you treat her as an adult, she is free to develop into a mature woman, and as such she is more capable of being a closer and responsive wife to you.

FOR FURTHER THOUGHT
Where Are You Now?
- In what ways does your leadership-attitude toward your wife reflect your regard for her as a person of high value (worth)?
- Ask your wife to read this chapter so you can discuss these ideas together:
  a. Do you agree or disagree that the biblical roles of the husband and the wife are given, not earned? Why?
  b. What are the implications of "equality with different function" in your marriage?

Where Do You Go from Here?
- List the strengths, gifts and abilities your wife has and decide on specific ways you will encourage and affirm these in her.
- Ask your wife to tell you honestly and lovingly what "parental phrases" or words you are using that she dislikes. Assure her that you will try to avoid these phrases in the future.

5
SO WHO'S PERFECT?

"He's always got to be right. He's never wrong. Even when he's wrong, he's right! Mr. Perfection. The last time he admitted a mistake was three years ago. Even then he was depressed for a week afterwards."

Marriage counselors in your town hear something very much like the above almost every day. It may be equally true for women, but most of us men find it hard to admit mistakes.

I Am What I Can Do
The reason we find it hard to admit mistakes is that most men get their feelings of self-worth or fulfillment from their performance. This is related most obviously

to our jobs. At a men's retreat in California a few years ago I asked a group of men to write their answer to this question: "What are you?" Almost all of them answered by giving their occupations or professions. "I am a teacher," "a banker," "a carpenter," were some of the responses. The answers were all something which was done. In effect they answered, "What are you?" by saying, "I do teaching," "I do banking," "I do carpentry work." Probably most of you would have responded similarly.

Many of you have known men like George. He was a successful businessman and always seemed happy with his life. Then he sold his business and retired at age 55 and suddenly had nothing to do. When he couldn't do the tasks he had always done, he became very unsure of himself. Weeks turned into months and lack of performance turned into self-doubt, self-doubt turned into a severe depression. With a loving wife and financial security to last for many years, he lost his will to live and aged physically at an unbelievable speed. At his funeral one of George's friends said to me, "I don't understand what happened, George always seemed to do so well." Without knowing it, that friend put his finger on the answer when he said "*do* so well." George had always been a doer. His self-confidence was based totally on doing.

Men go through this same emotional crisis when they are suddenly physically disabled. The shock of not being able to do what one used to do and finding some way to restore that sense of self-worth and confidence is, in many cases, a much bigger obstacle to hurdle than the physical adjustment.

Even with our sexual identification we tend to be performance-oriented. The other night I heard a man telling about a problem he was having of temporary impotence. He said, "I've not been able to be a man for three weeks." Was he suddenly a chicken? No, but his whole idea of manliness was based on his ability to perform rather than on any innate qualities of manliness or his state of being.

Our Perfection Standard

To make matters worse, the doing or performance we demand of ourselves is 100 percent perfection. It's a lot like the guy who high jumps 7 feet 2½ inches. If the bar was set at 7 feet 3 inches, his score is zero. You're a winner at 100 percent, but a failure at 99 percent.

When self-worth is based on performance, we spend most of our time trying to prove we're not failures, and to do that, we must be perfect. For most of us, our self-assessment rating bounces continually from 100 percent to zero percent and back to 100 percent with almost no stopping in between to give ourselves credit for an 89 percent or even a 39 percent performance. When your self-assessment is performance-centered, it demands that you be right all the time. Failure to be perfect is to be condemned to feeling like a zero. That's why we find it hard to see and admit our mistakes, even to ourselves, let alone to our children.

Ted's dad was someone who had to perform perfectly or at least convince himself that he was right, in order to avoid feeling like a failure. So whenever there was conflict in the home, Ted's dad had to come out on top. Problems were always someone else's fault. Ted was regularly criticized and blamed for things. His dad always gave him the feeling that he was really not quite good enough to be accepted. What did Ted do to feel better about himself? He tried harder and harder to perform perfectly, and it became harder and harder for him to face areas where he really was wrong.

47

When Ted became the head of a household, he used his authority to maintain his own delusion of perfection. He did so by putting down his wife and children. It's not hard to understand what is meant when the Bible says that the sins of the parents visit three and four generations.

Breaking the Cycle

Is there any way to break the cycle? I believe there is. The problem is continued from one generation to the next when children evaluate themselves in the same way that their parents evaluated them. Since none of us had perfect parents, all of us have adopted some imperfect assessments of ourselves built around the theme that if you are not perfect, you are not acceptable.

I once counseled with a girl, Marlene, who was utterly paralyzed with guilt feelings. At 21 she felt guilty for days about spilling the shampoo into the tub, and it was her shampoo and her tub. She was carrying around with her damaging and inaccurate self-evaluations acquired from excessively harsh, condemning parents. The way she was freed from those self-evaluations which demanded such perfection of her was to replace what her parents used to say about her with what the perfect parent, God, says about her. We can do this, too, saying the same things about ourselves that God says about us.

What God Says About Us

The first thing God says is that we are definitely not perfect. We have all fallen short of God's perfect standard (see Rom. 3:23). The second thing is that God loves us anyway. "While we were yet sinners, Christ died for us" (Rom. 5:8). And third, God's acceptance of us is not based on our being perfect but on our being His sons. We can be confident in that father-son relation-

48

ship. "(We) have not received a spirit of slavery leading to fear again, but...a spirit of adoption as sons" (Rom. 8:15).

The last time one of your children was really a problem, did you think of changing his name and making him move out of the house? Probably not. Your acceptance of him, as imperfect as he is, is ultimately based on his relationship to you. Even though sometimes you may foolishly give him messages that he's not quite good enough to be your son, the father-son relationship continues.

God's acceptance of us is certainly more consistent than our own acceptance of our loved ones. That's because God's acceptance isn't based on our inconsistent behavior. It is based on Christ's consistent behavior and our dependence on it.

To summarize, there are three biblical truths which form the only permanent basis for accepting ourselves even with imperfections. The first truth is simply that we *are* imperfect. God says that we have all fallen short of His perfect standard. Our experience validates this principle. We can readily see for ourselves that we do not perform perfectly.

The second truth is that God clearly does love us anyway. "While we were yet sinners He died for us" (see Rom. 5:8). The third truth is that God's acceptance of us is based on our believing in His Son, Jesus Christ, rather than on the basis of our performance.

Freedom from Perfection

It is a very freeing experience for us and our families when we no longer feel that we have to spend so much of our energy in self-centered activities or attitudes in quest of perfection.

We have discussed the servant-leader attitude in

previous chapters. We can actually have a servant attitude when we have accomplished the basic spiritual and emotional tasks of *admitting* and *accepting* our imperfection, *claiming* God's forgiveness and *believing* His acceptance. Seeing Christ more clearly, acknowledging His Lordship over us and making Him the center of our attention will produce precisely the results we are looking for: a spirit of humility, a servant attitude, and at the same time a sense of confidence and the ability to lead our households in a Christlike manner.

It is amazing to me, but true, that spiritual humility and a right understanding of God's total acceptance of us bring with them a solid basis for our own self-acceptance and confidence. On the other hand, feeling unacceptable, and trying to be acceptable by attempting to be perfect, makes us fearful, self-centered, and proud. Bending the knee and bowing the head to God lifts us up and makes us confident.

How is it that Christ was able to put aside being in the form (technically "formlessness") of God and take on the form of a servant as described in the Philippians 2 passage? He was able to let go of the form of godliness because He was totally confident that He was God. He didn't have to prove this with externals. If you and I could get a godly confidence, we could be freed from having to prove something, and we would be better prepared to take on the form of servants in our households.

Examine Your Own Standards!

Expecting unquestioning obedience from others is one sure sign that we are expecting perfect performance. When you notice traces of it in yourself, go back and see if you are operating on a performance basis again. When was the last time you were wrong, or apologized, or lost an argument? If it's been a while and because God says all your self-righteousness is as filthy rags, maybe you've slipped back into old habits. Other things to watch out for are having to have everything your own way, and sulking or throwing tantrums when you don't get your own way. This kind of behavior is expected in your three-year-old, but because it is immature and self-centered, it is not what your family needs from the servant-leader of the household. You will feel better when you meet your family's needs instead of your own.

There is another kind of self-centered behavior that is the flip side of the family tyrant. Rather than cause friction, or risk making a mistake, he makes no attempt to lead his family. He's more like the family pet. He focuses only on his own needs. When he comes home from work it is like having another child in the house. He involves himself in reading, or TV, or church, and virtually ignores the family. His wife ends up having to make most of the decisions and he has not had to get involved.

There is another thing to look out for here, and that is passing on perfectionist expectations to your children. Help them admit their mistakes. The best way is by modeling. When you notice you've got on one blue sock and one black sock, make a joke of it. Something like "Oops, Daddy made a mistake," and laughing heartily about it with your five-year-old will make it easier for her to be imperfect when she's 15. Incidentally, that was *your* mistake you can make an issue of, not hers.

FOR FURTHER THOUGHT
Where Are You Now?
• As leader in your home, how are you modeling for your family that self-worth is based on God's acceptance of the individual, not on standards of perfor-

mance? Check your response against Ephesians 2:9 and 2 Timothy 1:9.

- Examine your conversations with family members for the last week. When was the last time you admitted to your wife or children that you were capable of making a mistake or that you were wrong? When was the last time you made an apology, or lost an argument?

Where Do You Go from Here

- Prayerfully reread Romans 3:23; 5:8 and 8:15. Ask God to give you freedom from performance standards.
- Stop during your next several conflict situations and assess whether your ideas and demands are performance-centered or God-centered.

6
UNDERSTANDING YOUR FAMILY'S NEEDS

Darlene was a sweet gal who worked as a bank teller. She was an emotionally sensitive person. When she had difficulty balancing her accounts at the end of a day, she would begin to get nervous. The more nervous she became the less accurate she was. To make matters worse, her branch manager was harsh and demanding and used language Darlene had never before had directed at her. The more her boss yelled, the more upset Darlene became. By the time she arrived home in the evening, Darlene was emotionally exhausted.

Darlene's husband Dick asked my advice about what to do. "Darlene was crying about her job again last night, and about her boss yelling at her. I told her what she should do about it and why she didn't have to let that bother her, but it doesn't seem to help. She says that I don't understand her. It seems like the same thing happens at least once a week. What in the world does she want me to say?"

Dick's question is so common that, frankly, I doubt if any of us have been exempt from the frustration of trying to help our wives and children feel better and finding that they don't listen to us and they don't take our advice. When we've done everything we know to do, they still don't feel any better. Why don't they listen to us?

Doers and Be-ers

As men, when something is broken, we don't generally spend a lot of time thinking about what it feels like to be broken. When something is broken, we usually try to fix it. If something isn't operating properly, we probably try to find out why it isn't operating. Many of us get to the cause and do something about it. Generally, that's the way men are (this is consistent with the masculine performance-orientation discussed in previous chapters). We are "doers."

Wives do not generally think of themselves primarily as doers. They are be-ers. If we were to ask the "What are you?" question to our wives, we would not get as many performance-oriented answers as we did from the men. Women will more commonly respond, "I am a wife, a mother, a woman." These are not occupations, they are states of being.

If your family was planning a picnic and you see that the sky is cloudy, perhaps your wife would ask, "What will we do if it rains?" By asking this question your wife wants to convey to you that she is feeling worried because the happy, peaceful family time she was hoping to experience has been threatened by the weather.

56

You may not realize that your wife's question needs to be translated into a statement of her feelings or her state of being. You are likely to answer her question on a *doing* level with, "If it rains, we'll go inside or get wet." Your wife knows that already. She was trying to tell you about her state of being.

When a state of being person is hurt or embarrassed, she doesn't feel understood when her doing-oriented husband tries to "fix" the hurt or embarrassment. She is not even asking (believe it or not) for you to do something about it. She is not asking for specific instructions as to what to do to feel better (such as "take a walk," "take an aspirin," "find another job"). She most particularly does not want to be told that what she did or what she is feeling is wrong or dumb.

What Your Wife Wants

Your wife wants something from you which is really quite alien to your basic performance-oriented nature. She wants you to understand and care about what it is that she is being. If she is lonely, you are not really meeting her needs by telling her to go meet people. Her need is to know that *you* know she feels lonely, to know that you have some idea about what that must feel like, and that you're sorry she feels badly.

At one time or another, you may have said something to your children like, "Sorry doesn't get the garbage taken out," because you don't want them to talk about it, you want action. When your wife is upset, she is exactly the opposite. She doesn't want action. She wants to talk about it.

There are two basic principles that you can start applying when your wife is upset. These two principles, when applied properly, will help you communicate the love and concern that you have for your wife in a way that she will understand and in a way that will meet her needs.

Understanding

Your wife needs you to understand her state of being. Therefore the first principle is to tell your wife what you *think* she is feeling. The best way to know what she's feeling is to imagine what you would be feeling if you were her and in the situation which caused her to be upset. This helps you focus on her condition. This is not the same thing as telling her what you would have done in her circumstance (which is not what she needs).

Linda came home from the store in tears. "I'll never go back there again. I could have just died."

"What happened?" said Fred.

"I wrote a check to pay for the children's clothes and when the girl saw my name on the check she called the manager. My name was on a list of people not to accept checks from. The manager came out and all these people were standing in line while this guy told me I had written two bad checks in there. Then I said, 'No way was that me' and I started to cry. Finally the guy took me to his office to show me the checks. They were written by some girl with the same name as mine, but she has a different middle name and an 'e' in her last name. Then he was all apologies, but we were in his office and nobody heard him apologize to me. After that, he went out and yelled at the cashier. I'm never going back there!"

How do you respond to meet her needs in that situation?

a. Say it was just a mistake. It could happen to anybody. Don't worry about it.

b. Get mad and go see the manager.

c. Call a lawyer.

d. Tell her what she should have done.

e. Tell her God had a purpose in it.

f. None of the above.

The answer is "f," none of the above, because more than anything, she wants your understanding and these don't communicate understanding to her.

Here are some other possible responses.

a. Oh! That must have been awful.

b. You must have just felt like going through the floor.

c. I'll bet you felt like punching somebody.

Any of these responses would have been good. Notice in each of them, the speaker is telling her what he thinks she was feeling.

Caring

The second principle is that in addition to telling your wife what you think she's feeling, you can tell her how *you* feel about what she's feeling. Add your own feelings to your statements about her feelings, in the examples and you will add depth and warmth to your responses.

a. Oh! That must have been awful.

   I'm so sorry that it happened.

b. You must have just felt like going through the floor.

   I wish I could have been there with you.

c. I'll bet you felt like punching somebody.

   I certainly don't blame you.

When you don't know what to say, a pure caring response, by itself, isn't at all bad. "Oh, honey, I'm so sorry," is a good response.

If you tell your wife how you feel about her feeling when she is upset, only do so when what you feel is positive. If you think that her feeling is dumb, don't say that. Just stick to telling her what you think she is feeling until you do feel something positive. We will discuss when and how to share the negative feelings in the next two chapters.

Understanding Your Children

The principles which have been presented for understanding our wives are the same principles which apply for our children. Here are some examples of applying these same principles to problems of children:

"Oh, that must really hurt. Daddy's sorry that happened."

"It's hard to lose, isn't it?"

"It hurts when your friends don't act like friends, doesn't it?"

"I'm sorry Don broke your date. I know how that must hurt."

Tell them what you think they are feeling and tell them how you feel about their feeling. Particularly with young children, it's important that you get them to talk about their hurts and that you suggest a label for their feelings. They may not have an abstract vocabulary adequate enough to express, or even to know exactly what they are feeling. All they may know is that it feels very bad all over. By helping them find words that specifically label their hurts, you are giving them limits to the hurt. This helps them realize that it is not the whole world that has gone against them, just a certain situation or person. If they have a label for their feelings, they can handle them much better.

You may have heard your child say some of these general, all-inclusive statements, "Oh, I can never do anything right," or "Everybody hates me." If you can help them figure out what exactly is bothering them, they will feel a lot better than a generalized "everything is rotten."

If you see your child is greatly upset while trying to learn how to ride a bicycle or after striking out three times in a row, your label-response for their feelings might be something like one of these:

"It's disappointing when you don't learn things as quickly as you would like, isn't it?" or "It makes you pretty mad when you don't do things perfectly the first time, doesn't it?"

What to Avoid in Your Responses

Don't try to communicate instructions to your wife or child while they are hurting. Trying to teach at that time only accomplishes one thing. It communicates a lack of concern on your part. Since you are concerned, you need to show it in a way that will be understood. Avoid making comments like,

"Now why did you do that?"

"Won't you ever learn?"

"I told you to be careful."

Also avoid trying to convince, convict, or argue. If you are doing that, you are trying to move them from where they are to where you are without communicating to them that you really care about where they are. If you are trying to move them, you are focusing on your own point of view, and that's not the effective way to practice the understanding and caring response.

Avoid preaching and condemning. Stay away from even implying messages like, "That's a dumb feeling" or "You shouldn't feel that way." If they feel a certain way, then that's where they are, and telling them not to be there doesn't get rid of it. Even if their feeling really is a wrong feeling, they will have to look at it honestly, and feel your support of them personally, before they can let go of it.

In summary, if we are going to lead our wives and

children, we need to be aware of our tendency to focus on behavior and try to avoid a response to behavior patterns only. We can show our understanding by focusing on their condition of being and telling them what we think they are feeling.

FOR FURTHER THOUGHT
Where Are You Now?
- Think of two recent examples in which your wife was seeking emotional support from you for her statement of being. How did you respond?
- In what ways are you presently demonstrating the "understanding" and "caring" principles to your wife? To your children?

Where Do You Go from Here?
- Practice applying the understanding and caring principles in the emotion-laden situations that might arise in your family. Think about the responses you would make in the following possible situations:
    a. You come home to find your wife in tears. She tells you that she has dented a fender and scratched the door of the car. You respond by . . . .
    b. The Little League game is over. Your son's team lost by one point, and he was the one to make the final strikeout. You respond by . . . .

7
SPEAKING THE TRUTH IN LOVE

Marian came down the stairs all ready for church. "How do you like my new dress?" she asked.

John grinned broadly and said, "Oh I like it. It really looks good on you. It flatters you in every way. That's a good color for you."

John hated the dress. John also loves his wife and wouldn't hurt her feelings for anything, so he told her what he thought she wanted to hear.

On the other side of town, Luke and Dale were getting ready for church and Dale came out wearing her new dress. "Oh no! Not another purple dress. I can't believe it. The style of that thing makes you look 30 pounds heavier than you already are. You look like a grape."

These two couples illustrate one problem. "How do I tell my wife what's on my mind, when what's on my mind is not what she wants to hear?" We have demonstrated the two most common ways of handling this problem.

I Love Your Dress

The first way is simply to deny your negative feelings and say something loving. John's overly enthusiastic response to his wife does appear to be loving. Some would describe it as saccharin—artificially sweet. The main problem is that John was not truthful. He chose to be dishonest in order to be loving. Because of that, his wife doesn't really know how her husband feels about her dress, or how she looks in it. She may continue to wear the dress in order to please him because of his initial response. Meanwhile, he is becoming more and more bothered by her wearing something he hates. Both partners are trying to please each other, but there is a complete lack of understanding as to what the other one is really experiencing.

I Hate Your Dress

In the second example, Luke left little doubt in Dale's mind as to his true opinion of her dress. He was honest. He paid for it though. Dale was really offended by his response to her. The chances are also good that Luke will feel guilty about his outburst of honesty. Luke's problem was that his response was not loving.

Speak the Truth in Love

Ephesians 4:15 says, "Speaking the truth in love, we are to grow up in all aspects into Him, who is the head, even Christ." We can grow to be more Christlike, more like the head who is our model for headship by having two-pronged communication. One prong of the message is an honest statement of what is going on inside of you, whether it is a thought, or a feeling. The other prong is "I love you."

The "I love you" part of the message doesn't have to be said in these words, but the message needs to be clear. It's important to communicate this love, but it's also important to do it in your own words. Let your expressions be consistent with your own personality. I am convinced that there are ways to express love and concern which are, or can be, comfortable and quite possible for each of us. Some men are more verbal than others, but all of us can clearly communicate love and concern. God tells us to be loving (see Eph. 5:25) so it must be possible.

The following two examples may not fit at all with your personality, but they are illustrations of the principle of a two-pronged communication, pairing a negative impression about your wife's dress, with a positive opinion of her. For the sake of comparison, we'll use that same circumstance with the new dress.

Luke could have said, "Well, to tell you the truth, if anybody could save that dress from embarrassment it would be you." Or he could have said, "Honey, I will enjoy being with you in church today even if you do wear that dress."

There is a fine line here on which we must be careful not to lose our balance. "I love you even if that dress does make you look like the Goodyear Blimp" is the kind of thing that could be devastating to some women. Be careful not to make fun of her in the process of telling her that you love her anyway. The primary message that she must understand is your expression of love.

This two-pronged principle can be applied in almost every situation at home. When Jim woke up one morning he had no clean shirts or underwear. He reacted by feeling angry, but rather than start the day off yelling, he decided to keep it to himself. Jim was unusually quiet at breakfast time and went off to work with only a muttered, "See ya." He didn't call home all day. If our two-pronged communication system is applied to this situation, Jim can express his anger and therefore relieve it in the following manner.

When Jim comes home from work, he could go to his wife and say, "I was really angry with you this morning when I left for work because I had no clean shirts or underwear. All day long it felt like there was a wall between us and I hate that feeling. I wanted to tell you about it as soon as I got home so the wall could come down."

What did Jim just say? He said, "I've been angry at you all day," but he paired it with a message of "I love you" and it came through in a totally different way than it would have without the "I love you."

In summary, the two-pronged principle is based on Ephesians 4:15, "speaking the truth in love." Truth without love is selfish and painful to the receiver. Love without truth is dishonest. One prong of your communication is an honest expression of your feeling, and the other is a clear expression and genuine attitude of love.

FOR FURTHER THOUGHT
Where Are You Now?
- Decide why you agree or disagree with the statement that it is better to "speak the truth in love" to your wife than to deny your feelings about even the possible touchy matters.

Where Do You Go from Here?
- Using the principles in this and previous chapters of

the book, decide on at least two truthful, loving ways to respond to your wife in these situations:

a. Your wife had her hair cut. She likes it. You don't. She asks, "How do you like my hair?"

b. Your wife frequently has onions for lunch. She sometimes forgets to do anything about her dental hygiene. You notice this rather clearly when you kiss her hello.

c. Your wife and the furniture salesman both love a $700 sofa that you think looks like an explosion in a mattress factory.

8
DEALING WITH ANGER

In one week I had the following people come to my office: A pastor who was angry with his congregation, a patient who was angry with his doctor, a doctor who was angry with a patient, husbands who were angry with their wives, wives who were angry with their husbands, parents angry with children and children angry with parents. Whatever anger is, there's a lot of it going around.

What Is Anger?

When we analyze it, we find that anger is not a primary feeling. It is a reaction or a defense. This point can be illustrated by remembering times when as a boy you were wrestling or fighting. You and your foe stood there and hit each other as hard as you could, but you didn't feel much during the actual fight. It was after the fight, on the way home, that you began to feel the resulting bumps and bruises. As long as you were striking out, you didn't feel the pain. When you stopped striking out, you hurt. That is exactly what anger is, a virtually automatic reaction to an affront or attack of some kind.

This reaction may occur in several different kinds of circumstances. One kind of circumstance in which anger will occur is when you have been actively attacked, verbally or otherwise. If a car starts turning the corner just as you are stepping into the street to cross it, and the driver yells, "What's the matter with you, stupid!" you may react with anger. You got angry because the driver put a dent in your self-image.

You might also get angry if your neighbor comes over and punches you in the mouth. In this case it was not your self-image that was dented, it was your physical self. Both of these circumstances are examples of active attack.

Another kind of anger-arousing circumstance results when you have been passively attacked. Here no one comes at you directly, but your freedom of movement or your self-image is infringed upon in some way. Last month I was at a baseball game and a drunken college student continued to stand up directly in front of my view of the plate. I reacted by getting angry. I felt as though I deserved better treatment than that.

Another example of anger in a passive-attack circumstance is when we become angry if a traffic signal turns red just as we get to it. When these circumstances occur, we are asking some form of the question, "Don't they know who I am?"

We can say, then, that all anger of the kinds discussed so far is an aggressive, striking-out reaction from an attack on your real self or on your own image of yourself. We can go back to the illustration of the two boys fighting. Our mental rationale then was, "He hit me so I hit him back." When we feel actively or passively attacked by people, objects or circumstances, we react by wanting to strike back. This is anger. It is also worth noting that the original supposed attacker may not have intended any attack.

Is Anger Ever Righteous?

The Bible talks about an anger of a different quality, which we often call righteous indignation. In order to qualify as this type of anger, the motivation of the person involved is to be totally for the cause of Christ and His Church. This means he is to have no ego involvement whatever in the particular circumstance in which he is becoming righteously indignant.

Getting angry with sin is another way to look at righteous indignation. This is not a clear distinction, however. Many of us get angry at behaviors that are sinful. We may well be upset because the Christ who is our Saviour is being degraded by someone's practices. To the degree that such anger is having to do with my own self-image, it is not righteous indignation, it is just plain anger.

It is often difficult to separate these two kinds of anger. I remember a discussion among the elders and deacons, at a church where I attended, who became angry at teenagers talking during the church service. They came up with all sorts of plans which were intended to punish or embarrass or teach a good lesson to the teenagers. They felt what they thought was righteous indignation because the teenagers were talking in God's house and keeping people from hearing the gospel. The distraction factor was no doubt part of it, but how much of it was really just because the elders and deacons themselves were distracted? They were angered. They felt they deserved better treatment, more respect. While purely righteous anger theoretically exists, it would take a Christlike, selfless person to feel it without any of the other kinds of anger sneaking in.

Is Anger Sin?

We are defining anger as the defensive striking-out which occurs when one perceives that he or his image of himself has been attacked, hurt, dented, or disappointed. We are referring here to the emotion itself and not the expression of the emotion. Excluding purely righteous indignation from the discussion, we turn now to see whether anger is sin.

First, we see that anger seems to be automatic or innate. Children react with anger without ever having it taught them. If you have children of your own, you have heard your child, even as a small infant, get to a certain volume and kind of crying that was clearly different from an "I'm hungry" or "I'm wet" kind of cry. When you heard that cry, either you or your wife or someone who was visiting said, "He's angry."

Many children are taught to inhibit anger rather than express it. What kind of reaction would you have gotten if you had told your kindergarten teacher that you were angry at her? You know as well as I do that she wouldn't have put up with it. I remember to this day an incident in elementary school where a teacher said that I slammed a door because I was angry. She interpreted something she saw me do as anger and she made it clear that being angry was not acceptable behavior.

That same teacher, who holds a special place in my memory as being the one teacher least emotionally equipped to be in a room with 30 children, gave me an "F" on an otherwise perfect paper because I had rather stupidly forgotten to erase a picture I had drawn on the bottom of it that showed a grossly fat woman I had labeled "Teacher." Once again, the message I received was that whether in word, deed or drawing, anger or resentment were not to be expressed.

We are taught to deny its existence, but it is only

denial that is taught. The emotion does not need to be taught. It is already there. Does the innateness of this emotion give us any clear answers about the sinfulness of anger? I think that it does not.

Our old nature without Christ was certainly occupied with many sinful inclinations, but can we simply assume that the defense reaction of anger stems from our old nature? There are physical and emotional parts of us which do not seem common to either our old nature without Christ or our new nature in Christ. I choose to call these special parts our "natural" nature.

The natural nature would include our need for sleep and food, a need for emotional security, and needs for being accepted, loved and having a purpose in life. These needs cannot be rightly attributed to our new nature because they exist in everyone, regardless of their faith in God. Likewise these needs are not limited to our old nature because some of the needs will continue along with or as a part of our nature until in heaven they are ultimately and totally met in Christ.

Anger which is used to defend the physical and emotional self would seem to be part of our natural security operations, and as such, would be part of the natural nature and therefore not sin. This is the anger that you feel when someone comes at you with a knife, or when someone comes at you with a totally unfair attack on your character or motivation.

Defending the Self-Image

We turn now from the defense of the real self to the defense of the self-image. The self-image is how we feel about our own worth, our importance, and our performance.

Do you ever get angry when someone is pointing up your shortcomings, or something that you forgot? I know I do. We often do this even when we can see for ourselves that we have done something imperfectly. When someone points out that imperfection to you, he is attacking your self-image. As inaccurate and perfectionist as that self-image may be, if yours is attacked, you probably will get angry.

I remember painting a long hallway in an office building one Saturday. There wasn't much traffic in the building that day but there had been a little and someone had accidentally kicked an otherwise freshly painted, perfectly white wall. I had not yet repainted that place because I was by then at the other end of this hallway that was probably 150 feet long. Late in the day a lady came walking down the hall. Totally ignoring 150 feet of fresh white wall, she leaned over to the small kick mark about six inches off the floor and said, "Oh, what happened here?" I must confess I reacted by feeling angry and I told her I was. I knew that the hallway was not perfect, but when she told me about it, she was attacking my need to be perfect.

We have seen in previous chapters that while we may know better rationally, emotionally we often try to convince ourselves that we are functioning at 100 percent. Emotionally, we want to be right always; we want to believe we are very important, acceptable people in the eyes of others.

We have learned that an inaccurate self-image contradicts what God's Word says about us. God's Word says we are not perfect, so it is an inaccurate self-image which puts us in bondage to a standard of absolutely perfect performance, rather than absolutely perfect forgiveness. We can now see that anger becomes sinful when it is used to defend an inaccurate self-image because that inaccurate self-image doesn't say the same things about us that God does.

Can Anger Be Handled Positively?

All anger, even if it were not sinful in its origin, can be expressed sinfully. It would be sinfully expressed if it was unloving, judgmental, proud or self-centered. It is difficult to have an angry feeling and express it in a loving, accepting and humble way. Nevertheless, that is to be our goal. As soon as you realize that your emotional defense system is defending itself with the use of anger, check to see if that anger is defending the real you or the pretend, perfect, superior you. If that anger is coming from an inaccurate self-image, try to tell your self-image what would be a more accurate evaluation of who you really are. That will be getting to the cause of the anger. For example, when the traffic light turns red and you get angry, you might ask yourself, "Did you think you were so important that the light would stay green just for you?" Then regardless of which kind of anger you have (including righteous indignation), say what you are feeling, in a loving, accepting, and humble way.

Somebody just said, "Are you kidding? That's impossible and totally idealistic." You may be right, but we need a goal. One of my favorite statements is, "If you aim at nothing, you're likely to hit it." So we can at least aim at expressing our feelings in a more Christlike manner.

Wouldn't It Be Better to Just Deny Anger?

Denying anger, in order not to hurt people's feelings, is sin. The Bible says, "Do not let the sun go down on your anger" (Eph. 4:26). This means to deal with it quickly. It has been proven again and again that keeping anger inside does not make it die. It churns inside us until we express it.

Failure to express anger can cause various physical

ailments and intensify others. In addition to that, after building up several incidents which have made us angry, we are much more likely to explode in an uncontrolled outburst of temper.

I frequently counsel with a man who has a lot of trouble admitting and expressing his anger. When he feels slighted or taken advantage of, or put down, he usually turns and walks calmly out of the room. He doesn't talk about it to anyone. But that pressure cooker inside of him lasts only so long until it blows. Every few months he suddenly explodes at seemingly unimportant issues. When the explosion release occurs, he typically breaks the first piece of furniture he can put his hands on. He has hit his wife during these episodes, and she is now frightened to death of him. If he would express his angers one at a time when they happen, he could avoid these dangerous and dramatic explosions. He would have no reason for such behavior.

Another result of unexpressed anger is depression. Depression is a defense against anger just as anger is a defense against attack. Depression is directing anger in on one's self rather than out toward its original object. Ask any depressed person whom they are angry with and they will say they are angry at themselves. Don't believe them! They are directing that anger at themselves rather than directing it to others and risking rejection by them. Depressed people are not aware that they are doing this.

Sometimes people turn their anger in on themselves rather than expressing it because they have been told or led to believe that Christians don't talk about, or confess, or express their anger openly. They believe this in spite of their knowing that the Bible tells us to confess our faults to one another and to speak the truth in love.

Joel was 42 years old when he became a Christian. He

had never had any emotional illness and he had never been seriously depressed. After being around Christians who told him it was wrong to be angry and not to let that anger out, Joel stopped expressing his anger. Six months after he became a Christian, Joel entered a mental hospital with severe depression. We taught him to admit his anger rather than deny it, and we helped him learn some Christlike loving ways of expressing it. One month later he was back home and happy because he learned that even as a Christian, he needed to admit what he was feeling.

Shall I Say I'm Angry?

How does this basic need to constructively express our anger relate to us as heads of our homes? Let me suggest some ways.

The expression of anger can be the same, regardless of the type of anger. I suggest that you express it in your family as though it were confessing a fault. This will help your communication to be humble and accepting of others. Rather than saying, "You made me angry," you might say, "I felt angry when you did thus and so." This will help you accept the responsibility for your own feelings rather than blaming others.

Express your anger with words rather than with volume of sound. When you are starting to get angry with your child, say something like, "Now I'm starting to get angry because I've told you three times, and you still haven't done what I told you."

Anger is difficult to control. It can have a natural cause, or even a righteous cause, and yet can be expressed in a sinful way. On the other hand, it can have a selfish cause and can be expressed in a godly way. Regardless of the cause, when you realize you are angry, look for some loving, humble way to confess your anger.

Of course, keeping our focus on Christ can help us develop more and more the characteristics of a loving, servant-leader.

Once again, we find that seeing Christ more clearly helps us see ourselves more clearly. That gives us hope for a constructive expression and control of our anger in all situations, particularly in our families.

FOR FURTHER THOUGHT
Where Are You Now?

- Reconstruct at least two recent situations in which you became angry at your wife or a member of your family. Based on the information in this chapter, try to identify whether it was your self-image you were protecting in these situations or your physical or emotional self.

Where Do You Go from Here?

- Describe one other way you could have positively handled your feelings of anger in each of the two situations you identified above. Take further action to handle your anger positively in the future. The following suggestions will help you:
  a. Read James 1:19,20 to help achieve a spirit of humility so that you do not feel compelled to defend an inaccurate self-image.
  b. When your temper begins to flare, check to see if your anger seeks to defend the real you or the pretend, perfect you.
  c. Do not attempt to deny your anger, but deal with it quickly and constructively.
  d. Ask God to help you express in loving and humble ways the fact that you are angry and why.

PART II

ISSUES FACING LEADERSHIP IN THE HOME

9
THE GODLY MODEL

One summer morning an attractive young lady came to my office and said that she was having trouble praying. "I know the Bible says God loves me, but I just don't feel it. When I pray I feel as if no one is listening. When I ask God for something, I'm afraid He's mad at me for asking. I know I shouldn't feel this way, but I can't help it. That's the way I feel."

We have all heard about spiritual problems causing emotional problems and this certainly can and does take place, but in Cindy's case, she really believed that God cared and she really wanted God's best for her. Her problem seemed to be more of an emotional blockage which kept her from a fulfilled spiritual life. She couldn't feel God's love, even though she believed He loved her.

As we began to talk, it didn't take long before Cindy began to talk about her family life. She had a very hostile, self-centered and immature father who apparently did not care about Cindy or the rest of the family. As far as he was concerned, no one in the family ever did anything right except himself. If he said anything at all to Cindy, it was something angry or critical. Most of the time, he would simply not answer her at all. When Cindy was 10 years old, her father moved away. Left at home were Cindy's mother and six little children. The mother went on welfare because she received no money from her husband. At birthdays and Christmas Cindy would send cards to her daddy. He never answered.

After accumulating her background, I asked Cindy how she felt about her father now. She replied that she had always felt like a bother to him. She was quite sure by now that he didn't care about her, and she had given up trying to communicate with him.

Without being aware of it, Cindy had confused her feelings about God with her feelings about her dad. This is a natural, almost automatic thing to do. God presents Himself as a father figure to us. The Lord's Prayer addresses "Our Father who art in heaven" and we think of ourselves as His children. We call God our father when we pray and accept without question His presentation of Himself to us as our heavenly Father.

How does this father image of God affect us as heads of our homes? It affects us because we as earthly fathers are predetermining our children's emotional attitude toward God and their opinion of God's attitude toward them by our emotional relationship with our children. If we are always interested in their problem, ready to listen and willing to forgive, loving the child while disliking their misdeeds, then that is what our children will expect from God.

If, on the other hand, we are usually too busy to listen, if we tend to make promises and not keep them, if the only times we really notice or talk with our children are when they step out of line, then those are likely to be the responses they will expect from God.

Being a Godly Model Is Hard

Being the head of the house makes you, in many ways, the local representative of God in your house. Your wife is told to submit as to the Lord and your children are told to obey. I think they may have the easiest job. If my family is moving in the wrong direction, I will be the one to be held responsible. Family members are responsible to us as leaders and we are ultimately responsible to God.

Does this make you feel like giving up? Wait a minute before you do. Your modeling for your family what God is like is not something you have to decide you will or will not do. A model is something that you already are. You have already been modeling God to your children, and you may have been doing better at it than you think.

When one of my girls comes to me with tears in her eyes, a doll in one hand and the doll's arms in the other hand, I love being able to say, "Don't worry, Daddy will fix it." I have few joys in life that are any greater than touching broken toys and making my little ones happy by fixing the things that cause them problems. I'm sure most of you react the same way.

God is like that. He is pleased when we come to Him with our broken lives and ask Him to touch them and make them better. We demonstrate this truth to our children when we are pleased that they trust us with the little broken things in their lives and respond to meet their needs.

When our children are hungry and ask us for food, do

we get angry and give them a snake to eat, as Luke 11:11 asks? No, we want to provide for them.

If an eight-year-old asks for a bicycle, what father, if he can afford it and believes it beneficial for the child, wouldn't give this little extra thing that makes life more enjoyable?

As father-leader, you demonstrate God's provision and His grace everytime you give to your children. This demonstration of God's grace is something you are already doing every day. I don't wish to frighten you into doing something you've never done before. I want you simply to realize what you are *already* doing, to be aware of the implications of your behavior. And again, I would like to reinforce you by stating that many of those behaviors are just fine.

We have already seen that God's model of leadership is servanthood. We can probably all agree that servanthood is not doing what comes naturally. There are some readers who are wondering, "If I put all my energies into leading the family, meeting my children's needs and my wife's needs, who meets my needs. Aren't my needs important?"

The answer to that question is that your needs are important, but they are not your responsibility. They are for your wife to meet. They are for God to meet. It is your responsibility to communicate what your needs are, but not to meet them. God's plan is that you communicate your needs and meet your wife's. Meanwhile, she tells you what she needs (it is not your responsibility to guess) and she in turn meets yours.

The "communication of need" principle may be demonstrated by the following example. Charlie comes home from work. He is exhausted. When he walks in the door, he comes face-to-face with a lot of needs. His children need some attention, his wife needs some peace, the grass needs to be mowed, etc. Charlie says to his family, "I'm really exhausted, I have a headache that won't quit. I feel if I could lie down for a half-hour I could face the evening." Charlie has communicated a need.

What happens next depends on whether Charlie is meeting his own needs or whether his wife is meeting them. If Charlie is meeting his own needs, he would probably say, "I'll be lying down, call me when dinner's ready." Charlie has given himself the privilege of lying down rather than playing with the children or meeting some other need of his family.

If his wife is meeting his needs, then she would say, "Why don't you lie down. I'll call you when dinner is ready and I'll keep the children downstairs." When that nap is given to you as a gift from your wife in this way, the nap is infinitely better than when you decide to take it for yourself.

The Godly Model Meets Needs—Regardless

There is one other category to speak to and that is, "What happens if I don't take the rest for myself and my wife doesn't give it to me as you have described?" The answer is that you go meet the needs of the family by playing with the children. "Even with a headache?" Yes, even with a headache. It is certainly true that in areas of health we have a certain responsibility to take care of our own bodies, but the point is that your primary responsibility as the head of a house is to meet the needs of the people in your family, whether you feel like it or not.

It may seem to be somewhere between difficult and impossible to put our family's needs above our own, but that is what Christ did for us, and that is what we are to do for our families. How? By knowing God better, by being aware of our responses to our families. By putting their needs above our own, we are modeling what God has done for us through Christ.

Much of the godly-attitude modeling comes by way of a fairly natural process. When a father really cares about his children, the children are learning about a caring-father figure. The more you become aware of this the better you'll become at being a godly model, a caring-father figure to your children.

FOR FURTHER THOUGHT
Where Are You Now?
- Make an adjective "picture" of the ideas your children have developed about God, the heavenly Father, from the example you have set as their earthly father (Example: judgmental, forgiving, etc.).
- What attitudes and feelings toward God are you consciously trying to encourage in your children?

Where Do You Go from Here?
- Evaluate your adjective picture of God. What are the positive attitudes and actions you wish to strengthen as your children's earthly model of God? What are the negative attitudes and actions you wish to delete as destructive to this model?

10
YOU AND YOUR CHILD'S SEXUALITY

In chapter 9 we discussed the effect that fathers have on their children's attitude toward God. We move now to discuss the critical role fathers play in the development of their children's sexuality and sexual understanding.

Your Child's Sexual Understanding

It is important that each of our children grow to understand the significance of their own sexuality as well as the basics of the reproductive process. Each child has a normal curiosity about these topics, so questions will probably come up quite naturally as our children notice differences between boys and girls, or between mother and dad.

"The less they know about sex, the less likely they will

be to get into trouble," is the attitude of many fathers who cop out of their responsibility for training their children in sexual understanding. Unfortunately, this attitude almost guarantees that our children will have distorted sexual concepts because it prompts us to 1. look embarrassed when our children ask questions or show curiosity about sex; 2. make our children feel guilty for wondering about their bodies; and 3. fail to answer our children's questions with simple and accurate information.

These kinds of reactions teach our children not to ask us *anything* about sex and cause them to believe there is something embarrassing or unnatural about it. As a consequence, we leave our children's sex education to the muddled and secular impressions they receive from their playmates. Playmates are not qualified to teach our children about sex in the context God planned it. We are!

As father-leaders, we are responsible for the sexual education of our children. Our wives will aid and support us greatly in this task, but the final responsibility is ours. Giving our children books to read and sending them to read these books alone is abdicating our responsibility for their sexual education as well as robbing us of a valuable father/child sharing time. Going through an appropriate book and talking about its content together can be a wholesome and informative experience for dad and child alike. In this procedure, a father gives more than just information; he also gives himself.

Some fine books have been written for us about what, when and how much to tell our children about sex. At this point, I prefer to suggest a few good ones in the "For Additional Reading" section at the end of this book and go on here to enlarge on an important aspect of our children's developing sexuality: sexual identification.

Sexual Identification

This may be a sensitive topic for some people, but I thought you would want to know how parents sometimes make their children homosexuals. Unless there is something to stop them, boys learn about being a man by modeling themselves after their dads. This is called identification. Likewise, girls learn to become women by identifying with their mothers.

Part of learning to be a man is, of course, becoming attracted to women, and part of learning to be a woman is becoming attracted to men. If mother and dad have a decent relationship and both parents are reasonably accepting of their children, the sexual identification process is carried off quite naturally. The child doesn't even know it is taking place. But, problems can arise which block the natural process. We need to look at these problems so we can learn to avoid them in our own families.

Overly Critical Fathers

An overly critical, condemning father can cause problems for both boys and girls. Boys whose dads are constantly putting them down and harshly criticizing them find it difficult to want to be like dad. They are afraid of him, and are much more comfortable under the support and protection of mother rather than enduring the constant barrage of father. These boys gradually begin to identify with mother. They don't want to be like dad. As far as they are concerned, dad is mean all the time. When a boy begins to identify with his mother, he notices that she is attracted to men and, ultimately, so is the boy. To avoid this, you need to be accepting of your son. Also, you need to be the kind of person your boy is comfortable being with.

Mike taught social studies in high school and coached

the junior varsity football team. One of the happiest days of Mike's life was the day his wife gave birth to their son. Just like on television, Mike went out that day and bought a football for his son, Mike Junior. It was very important to Mike that his son grow up to be strong and tough. Every time the baby cried, Mike felt that somehow little Mike was too soft. He made it his personal project to toughen up the little guy. As Mike Junior grew up, every time he cried, dad called him a sissy. Mike Senior criticized and condemned.

One of the worst times of Mike's life was the day he found out that little Mike had a natural gift for drawing and enjoyed painting and mixing colors more than competitive sports. The harder dad pushed his son, the less the boy wanted to have anything to do with dad. Michael didn't want to grow up to be like his dad. Today he is a homosexual. It was not his fondness for drawing and other artistic expression that made him so. It was his dad's unaccepting attitude toward him which never allowed Michael to really want to identify with or be with dad.

Overly critical dads can make it hard for girls to love them. Normal little girls, in their process of identifying with mother, fall in love with their daddy. If they can't love dad, it becomes hard for them to love other men when they grow up. They tend to expect the same kind of treatment from all men that they received from dad. If dad was loving and caring, they will expect this same loving attitude from other men. If dad was harsh and condemning, they will expect that.

An adult woman who was never able to love her dad is apt to be hostile to all men. She may deal with this by moving into the lesbian community and simply writing off men as nonexistent.

An alternative way of dealing with this hostility to

men is for the woman to marry someone she can push around, someone for whom she can make life miserable. Also, many sexually promiscuous women are promiscuous because they feel as though they can control men in this manner.

Overly Critical Mothers

The application of these dynamics is virtually the same with an overly critical mother. A little girl can't identify with a hateful or condemning mother. I have been working with a girl named Toni for many months. Toni is a lesbian. Her mother was a very religious woman whose life was centered around the word "should." Everything Toni ever asked or told her mother received a "should" or a "shouldn't" reply. Toni was never given the chance to love her mother. Whatever attempts she made to try to win her mother's favor were met with condemnation. Finally Toni gave up. Now she would rather be anything than to be like mother.

A little boy with a condemning mother can become so angry that he could never love any woman because mother was the first woman he knew and he hated her. Sid hates his mother. He has hated her since she threw his dad out of the house so that she could live with the next door neighbor. He hated her because she never gave him a compliment and because she spent every dime she could find on clothes for herself. When Sid was five years old, she would send him out to play at 8:00 A.M. and lock the door. Often she would not let him back in the house until after dark, leaving him to fend for himself. Sid still hates his mother. He doesn't have any friends who are women. He doesn't trust women because of his initial experiences with his mother. Sid is a homosexual.

Sex and Spiritual Leadership

As spiritual leaders of our homes, we are responsible not only for giving our children information about sex, but also for educating them to its God-ordained purposes. We fathers are to instruct our families in biblical values as well as in the facts of sexuality and sexual behavior. The scriptural teachings on sex standards are scattered throughout the Bible. The undergirding principles for fathers striving to be good models to their children is probably 1 Corinthians 6:19,20:

Do you not know that your body is a temple
of the Holy Spirit who is in you, whom you
have from God, and that you are not your
own? For you have been bought with a price:
therefore glorify God in your body.

Without moral instruction and modeling based on this passage, along with factual information, we are not realistically preparing our children to face sexual responsibility as Christian adults.

We stated earlier the importance of children being able to identify comfortably with their parents. Children need a clear view of each sex as a basis for their behavior as male or female for they learn much about their sexuality by observing our attitudes and actions as men who are husbands and fathers and by observing our wives as women and mothers. Equally important is their need for a clear view of their sexuality from a Christian viewpoint.

Our modeling of what a worthy man is like in his attitudes and relationships to women is vital for our daughters. They need us as contrasts to their femininity *and* as godly models. Our modeling of our attitudes and relationships with women and also how we may glorify God in our bodies is vital for our sons.

In the final analysis, fulfilling our obligation as the

primary sex educators for our families is not a simple matter. It is a difficult task and it must be accomplished in a society of rapidly shifting sexual values. Ultimately, our success or failure as father-leaders will not be measured by what we achieve in the sex education of our children, but rather in the total atmosphere we create in the home and in our whole relationships with our children.

FOR FURTHER THOUGHT
Where Are You Now?
- Evaluate your impact thus far on the developing sexuality of your children according to the following questions:
  a. Am I providing adequate and appropriate sex information as my children request or need it?
  b. Am I providing moral instruction with a biblical perspective along with factual information?
  c. Am I providing a strong, mature father image that would be an appropriate contrast to my daughter's femininity and a good model for my son's masculinity?
  d. Am I showing tender concern and respect for their mother at all times?
  e. Am I being too critical or authoritative in the demands I make of my children?

Where Do You Go from Here?
- Read Deuteronomy 6:5-9 together with your wife. Discuss with your wife how you can enhance your children's sexual identification with the husband-father role. Use your answers to the questions above as guidelines.

11
DAD AND CHILD DISCIPLINE

The primary objective of parenting is to produce a confident, independent adult. Parents haven't failed if their child gets a punch in the nose or makes a mistake. Parents fail when their children remain children.

Children are, of course, not ready to assume adult responsibility until they are adults. It would be a mistake to force them into independence before their time, but we do need to have independence in mind as our ultimate goal.

Freedom Within Boundaries
The way to prepare children for adulthood without overwhelming them with more than they can handle is by providing freedom within boundaries. The benefits of this system are many. By being able to make choices, the

child develops a sense of individuality that is very important in later life.

The whole purpose of adolescent rebellion is to assert one's individuality and independence from parents. If parents encourage enough personal choice before their child's teenage rebellion time, there will be little reason to rebel. I am suggesting that we can at least reduce this adolescent turmoil with the use of freedom within boundaries.

Basically, freedom within boundaries means allowing a child to do whatever he chooses among options or within limits which you set. If teen rebellion is going to be softened, the best time to start giving controlled freedom is by the time your child is two.

How much freedom can a two-year-old handle? Probably not very much, but you can hold up two pairs of pajamas and ask the child, "Do you want to wear these red pajamas or these blue ones." It doesn't really matter in the long run which he wears, so why not let him choose? The reason most of us don't allow choices is that it takes a few seconds longer to pull out two pairs of pajamas than to pull out just one pair and say, "Wear these."

In this case, no matter which pajamas the child chooses, he is equally safe, warm and healthy. I would not let a two-year-old decide whether or not to wear pajamas, because that could possibly affect his health by letting him catch cold. That would be a consequence of his choice that I am not ready for him to bear yet. When he is 16 he can bear that consequence and that would be different, but right now he can bear the responsibility of choosing red over blue, so I can let him choose that.

Likewise, I would not let my five-year-old decide whether or not to have breakfast, but I would let her decide what she would prefer to eat for breakfast, within certain limits. Cake, popcorn, or ice cream are outside the limits of breakfast, based on what I believe to be her nutritional needs.

The general rule of thumb is that if a child is ready to bear the consequences of his decision or choice, then I can let him make that decision for himself. Freedom without limits is not disciplining at all, it is not even love. As the father, you may know or believe certain things to be unhealthy for your child. You have both the right and the responsibility to set the child's limits regarding these things.

Because a five-year-old can handle more freedom and responsibility than a two-year-old, and a twelve-year-old more than a six-year-old, the trick is to be constantly aware of your child's growth and capabilities and keep expanding his limits, just ahead of him. Keep coming to him and saying something like, "Now I think you are ready to make this decision or that decision for yourself."

It Is Hard to Let Go

It is often difficult to watch our children liking different things than we like. Sometimes your daughter may choose the red pajamas when you would like her to wear the blue. Your son may join the chess club instead of the wrestling team. When we feel such frustrations, it would be a good time to remind ourselves that we are here to meet our children's needs. *They are not here to meet ours.*

You are bound to make a few mistakes along the way, but at least you can be actively working toward creating a confident, independent adult, rather than someone you can control all his or her life. You wouldn't want permanent control even if you had it. Nevertheless, it is surprising how many parents, mostly mothers, find it difficult to let go of their children and to initiate positive action to usher their children gradually into adulthood.

I have noticed that when adults have residual feelings toward their parents, the feeling that almost always exists toward mothers is anger. I have become convinced by repeated observation that the anger is due to a mother's trying to control or to mother her grown child when that child no longer needs or appreciates mothering.

Residual feelings toward fathers are totally different. When there are leftover feelings about fathers, they almost always contain a message like, "Why didn't you give me more limits?" or "You never showed any affection to me," or "The only times you ever noticed me were when I was bothering you." The love and acceptance of a father is necessary for the emotional well-being of the son or daughter. Without it, it is very hard for children to develop a sense of individuality, confidence, and security.

Disciplining in Dad's Absence

We have tried to make the message clear that the father's supervision and presence in discipline, as well as all other areas of family life, are vitally important. That supervision and direction can be given even when dad is not home.

While dad is at work, children can still be responsible for chores which dad said for them to do. When your children become teenagers, it is more important than ever for the parental expectations and limits to come from dad. When children come home from school, mother can simply say, "Remember your dad said to do the lawn before he gets home."

While teenage girls definitely need their dads' affection and influence in their lives, it is debatable whether teenage girls need their dads to do a lot of the daily, small-issue kinds of disciplining. Teenage girls in general seem to respond about as well to their mother as to their father. It seems to depend on the particular family and the particular girl whether she responds more positively to one parent or the other. In any case, the principles given below apply for daughters as well as for sons.

When boys start to become men, some mothers have a difficult time disciplining them. Their father is strongly needed in these situations to move in and reinforce the mother's discipline and, if necessary, take over even the minor problems of disciplining. Whether it is right or not, the fact exists that boys get a message that boys are better than girls and that men are better than women. When boys start to feel like men, they realize that mother is a woman, and some of them are not really about to let a woman tell them what to do. From their point of view, it puts their newfound manliness in question if they obey a woman.

If your wife becomes frustrated as she tries to maintain the respect and discipline of her teenage boy, I suggest that in this situation the father do most or virtually all disciplining of the boy. When you are not home, your wife needs to have enough specific directions from you to discipline *in your name* by saying "Dad said so and so." What if your boy doesn't obey when mother reminds him of what dad's orders were? Your wife needn't argue or struggle with your son over this. Other than telling you what happened, she does not need to do anything. The problem becomes a matter between you and your son. It was your word he was disobeying, and you can deal with him about that as well as for being disrespectful to his mother later.

Women who have always been sweet and patient

103

sometimes become angry and nagging women when their teenage sons don't obey them. I suggest you may want to prevent this from happening and at the same time prevent your son from having a reservoir of residual anger at mother. You can do this by becoming very active in the discipline of your teenage son. It will depend on your particular family, but you may need to become just as active with your daughter. Your discipline and direction are important for each of your children and at all ages.

Help Your Wife Assign Responsibilities and Limits

Perhaps a word is in order about what kinds of specific instructions are necessary to leave so that your wife can discipline in your name. Hopefully there will not be many that are needed by the time your children are teenagers. You don't want to be running every minute of their day. Most of your directions will fall into one of two categories: responsibilities and limitations.

Responsibilities mean letting your children know what is expected of them. For most families these responsibilities will be either related to school or the household and family. School responsibilities are primarily doing homework. If you handled this extremely well before your children were teenagers, and if they enjoy their studies, you may never need to talk much about this; but for most families there are times when parents feel the children need some help in structuring this area. You may need to require that your child work a certain number of hours each afternoon or evening on homework. Some parents require that homework be done before children go out to be with friends; others require that it be finished before watching television.

Household and family responsibilities would include keeping one's room neat, mowing the lawn, washing the car, doing the dishes, etc. I interviewed several young adults whom I considered to be well put together emotionally. They were mature, had good work records, and continued to have good relationships with their parents. One of the things that virtually all of them said was that their parents gave them responsibility early in life.

One young lady said that her dad put her in charge of the family car maintenance. She took it for inspections, oil changes and watched and waited while it was being fixed. She remembers this as one of the best things that happened in her life to teach her responsibility.

The second category in which you will want to leave specific instructions is in the area of limitations. Once again the general rule is the fewer limitations the better. We must give our children the chance to make mistakes if they are going to learn from them and learn how to cope with them. I know a man who falls apart when he makes a mistake. He can't handle it. Why can't he? Because his parents so sheltered and controlled his life that he didn't have any practice at coping with failure and frustration. Their oversheltering his life turned him into an emotional cripple.

Though you should limit the parental restrictions you place on your children, some are definitely necessary. These change with the age of the child; the older the child, the fewer restrictions necessary. Many parents find it necessary to limit the amount of television that their children watch and some also limit or control which television shows the children may see. I think these are probably both very appropriate, but still you should try to give freedom within limits whenever possible. I remember my parents allowed me to watch only one-half hour of television before supper when I was in grade school. However, they did allow me to pick which half-hour I would watch.

Other limitations you may feel necessary to include in your discipline plan might include where children may or may not go, and with whom they may play. Picking your children's associates is tricky business. It is an intrusion on their personal life-style and a parent had better have a good reason for such an intrusion.

There is one particular person with whom I will not let my oldest daughter associate. My wife and I could see repeated instances of my daughter's behavior being negatively affected by this person. We are glad we made this difficult decision, and we are also glad we didn't just make it on impulse. We thought it through beforehand and explained it to our daughter. She wasn't happy about it, but I think she understands and she may even appreciate it some day.

Tips from Successfully Parented Adults

I referred above to interviews and group discussions with adults who have been, in my opinion, successfully parented by virtue of the fact that they are responsible adults who have gained some independence from their parents, but who also respect their parents. Here are the main points made by this sample group.

1. *Start early.* The first thing most of them said was that there was little disciplining necessary as teenagers because by that time they knew when their father said something, he meant it, so they did it. They all said that they knew their father loved them and also that he had been strict in their early years. They saw him as someone who said what he meant, meant what he said and didn't make idle threats.

This contrasts quite strongly with the parents who come to me with rebellious teenagers whom they have found they can't control. These parents usually gave few limits to the children when they were young. The parents let them do pretty much whatever they wanted as they were growing up. Then when the child started going wild as a teenager, they tried to clamp down on them. This tactic almost never works. Be strict early and then ease up gradually as the children are growing up.

Children know what idle threats are. If you say, "Finish your meat or you can't have cake for dessert," and give the cake without them having finished their meat, then you are doing the opposite of what successfully parented children respect in their parents.

2. *Listen.* The other major point that our sample group made was that their father listened to them. Listening takes time. You will need to be available. If your daughter is doing the dishes, how about sitting down in the kitchen, or even better, do them with her instead of reading the paper. If your son is washing the car, be there. Incidentally, I do not mean to imply in the previous two sentences that responsibilities need to be made along sex-typed roles. I washed dishes every night for several years. It didn't hurt me a bit.

3. *Give them your time.* Along with listening and availability, the happiest childhood memories for these folks were times alone with their parents, particularly with dad. Some went to the store together, one rode along with dad when he made seed deliveries to farms, one went on walks in the woods with dad. They also said that even when they weren't talking, they were together and that was the important thing.

It doesn't matter if you have six children or two or one. Make time to be alone with each one. Significantly none of the sample group listed family times as their richest memories, as important as family times may be. Relationships are not built in groups. They are built in pairs.

4. *Avoid comparisons.* As an afterthought, most of

the people agreed that they didn't like being compared to other brothers and sisters. One told of a parent who went in to talk to the first-grade teacher to make her stop referring to an older sibling.

5. *Don't yell.* Finally, the sample group agreed that being yelled at was totally unnecessary. Yelling only produces anger and fear and is damaging to your children's self-images and your own image as father-figure. When an increasing volume of sound is required in your directives to produce action, your children quickly learn to "tune you out." Your communication with your children also suffers as they take measures to avoid these loud and uncomfortable confrontations. Saying what you mean in a firm, clear voice and following through, if necessary, produces respect.

FOR FURTHER THOUGHT
Where Are You Now?
- Evaluate your present discipline plan as objectively as possible. Use the following questions to aid you:
  a. Do I allow my child to make personal choices within the limitations of his age and abilities?
  b. Do I frequently consider whether or not my child is ready for more freedom and responsibility?
  c. Do I give my wife specific directions for disciplining in my name during my absence?
  d. Do my wife and I assign responsibilities and limits?

Where Do You Go from Here?
- Make a list of specific ways you can provide better discipline boundaries for your children based on your answers to the questions above and the "Tips from Successfully Parented Adults" in this chapter. Resolve to diligently put these into practice as you seek to discipline your children.

12
HOW TO END ARGUMENTS

If we really did everything we knew to do to end arguments, we would probably be living "happily ever after" and this chapter and others in this book would be unwritten and unread. Somehow, though, we go on making the same mistakes we thought we had learned about and left behind. We get tired, or short of money, or under some other stress, and again we end up in the middle of an argument with our wives.

Jesus, our servant-leader model, responds to the subject of conflict in the Beatitudes where He teaches, "Blessed are the peacemakers; for they shall be called sons of God." The third chapter of James further emphasizes the importance of the peacemaker and notes the need for a heavenly wisdom. Verses 17 and 18 of

James 3 describe the qualities of wisdom inherent in the peacemaker.

> But the wisdom from above is first pure, then peaceable, gentle, reasonable, full of mercy and good fruits, unwavering, without hypocrisy. And the seed whose fruit is righteousness is sown in peace by those who make peace.

So, how can James 3 be translated into your life to lift you out of the conflict cycle? The first step is to stop mid-argument and listen to yourself. You will probably hear yourself saying something like, "My point is . . . ," or "You're not listening to me . . . . " Whatever you hear yourself saying, your purpose will be to try to prove that you were or are right. We saw in earlier chapters that we have a need to be right when our self-concept is based on our performance instead of God's acceptance of ourselves.

If you stop to analyze your attitude in the middle of an argument, you will see that your whole focus of attention is on yourself. That is how you got into the argument trap; both you and your wife are defending your own self-images.

The next question is how do you end an argument once it has begun. What we need to do at this point is change the focus of our attention from our own point to our wife's viewpoint. A basic rule of conflict is that as soon as one partner stops saying, "But my point is . . . " and starts saying, "I see your point is . . . ," the argument is well on its way to being over.

Learning to listen may really sound like a pat answer, but most marital arguing is nothing but selfish defensiveness. If one of you begins to really listen and tune into the other partner, the listening person is not being selfish or defensive. When communication opens up with one partner communicating and the other partner being communicated to, the threatened partner soon realizes he or she is not being attacked and can stop being defensive.

Different Perspectives

Any two people are different. They will have different backgrounds and experiences, different educational histories, different personality traits, different abilities, different habit patterns, and on and on. You already know that. For some reason, even though we know people are different, we have a tendency not only to expect, but even insist that other people see things our way.

I am reminded of the story of the blind men who were taken to "see" an elephant for the first time. One man touched the tail and said, "An elephant is like a piece of rope." Another man touched a leg and said, "Oh no, an elephant is like a trunk of a tree." The third man put his hands on the elephant's side and said, "You're both wrong, an elephant is like the side of a house." A great argument arose among them to find out which was right.

Who really was right? For the blind men the only way to a correct answer was for them all to hear the other men's perspectives and accept each as valid. By pooling their various perspectives they came up with a composite and more accurate perspective together than did any one of them singly.

The situation with our wives is often similar. By focusing totally on our own particular viewpoint of something, and by not accepting any other viewpoints as possible, we often seem as foolish as the blind men narrowly making judgments with only the perspective of touch.

So Who Gives In?

Assuming that you agree with me when I say that as

soon as one person shifts his focus from himself to his partner the argument is near completion, then who should be the one to give in first?

"Because she's my wife, she should submit and give in to me," is one opinion.

Well now, before we accept that opinion, let's review for a minute. Who is the head of the house?

"The husband."

What did Christ mean by leadership?

"Being the primary servant to meet the needs of the people for whom you are responsible."

Good, and what are your wife's needs when you and she are arguing?

"She needs to be straightened out?"

No. She needs to be understood and know that her opinions and perspectives on things are worth listening to. Because you are her primary need-meeter, you are the one to shift your focus and listen first to what your partner is really saying.

By your willingness to listen to your wife's perspective, you are supporting her self-image, keeping communication lines open, and, most important, showing her that you care about her as a person.

After you have listened deeply and carefully to her feelings, you can communicate, in love, your own feelings to your wife. Your role as peacemaker lies in first hearing your wife and accepting her as she is, not in building further hostilities. As peacemaker/leader in your home, the final decision is your *responsibility*, not your *right*.

FOR FURTHER THOUGHT
Where Are You Now?
• Write your answers to the following questions:
  a. How are arguments usually handled in your home?

b. Is it important for you always to be right?

c. Does your wife feel free to voice her opinions?

d. Who usually gives in to end the argument—you or your partner?

Where Do You Go from Here?

- Prepare yourself to play the role of peacemaker the next time an argument begins. Practice the following guidelines in the conflict situation below:

  a. Listen to yourself mid-argument to determine your focus of attention.

  b. Listen to your wife and strive to keep communication lines open.

  c. Be objective about your wife's viewpoint.

  d. Show her you care about her as a person.

  e. Assume your responsibility to end the argument.

Conflict Situation: You do not believe that wives should work outside the home. Your wife has just expressed a desire to go back to work. Before you both realize what has happened, a heated argument has erupted.

13
THE GREATEST OF THESE IS LOVE

Paul draws a beautiful portrait of love in 1 Corinthians 13:

> If I speak with the tongues of men and of angels, but do not have love, I have become a noisy gong or a clanging cymbal. And if I have the gift of prophecy, and know all mysteries and all knowledge; and if I have all faith, so as to remove mountains, but do not have love, I am nothing. And if I give all my possessions to feed the poor, and if I deliver my body to be burned, but do not have love, it profits me nothing. Love is patient, love is kind, and is not jealous; love does not brag and is not arrogant, does not act unbecomingly; it does not seek its own, is not provoked,

does not take into account a wrong suffered, does not rejoice in unrighteousness, but rejoices with the truth; bears all things, believes all things, hopes all things, endures all things. Love never fails; but if there are gifts of prophecy, they will be done away; if there are tongues, they will cease; if there is knowledge, it will be done away. For we know in part, and we prophesy in part; but when the perfect comes, the partial will be done away. When I was a child, I used to speak as a child, think as a child, reason as a child; when I became a man, I did away with childish things. For now we see in a mirror dimly, but then face to face; now I know in part, but then I shall know fully just as I also have been fully known. But now abide faith, hope, love, these three; but the greatest of these is love (1 Cor. 13).

Love is the most important ingredient in our roles as servant-leaders. If we seek to reflect Paul's beautiful portrait of love in our marriage relationships, we will make our wives happy, provide a warm and encouraging environment for our children and bring personal fulfillment to our own lives.

How do we go about attaining such love? The following are 10 principles that we can endeavor to apply to our marriage relationships to attain this love and at the same time fulfill our other obligations as servant-leaders. These principles are both a summary to this book and a challenge to each of us as leaders in our homes.

1. *Make your wife's happiness a top-priority goal.* If you ask some husbands "What are your chief goals in life?" they will answer "To be a foreman at work," or "To have financial security," or "To serve the Lord and

become more like Christ." Many can list their top 10 goals in life and not have their wife's happiness as one of them. We have to plan how we can achieve our goals and take specific steps to reach them. If we want to make our wives happy, we need to think of this as a goal and plan accordingly. We may not make them happy very often if we only do it by accident.

2. *Desire to improve your marriage.* This second point is somewhat similar to the first, but it focuses on the marriage as a whole rather than on your wife as an individual.

A marriage relationship is something like sitting in a rowboat in the middle of a river. You can't settle for the status quo and rest on your present relationship as good enough. If you lie back and rest your oars to enjoy where you are, it won't be long before the current has moved you downstream. You must exert effort in your marriage just to keep it in the same place as it was yesterday. If you want it to be better, that will take twice as much effort.

3. *Be courageous.* It takes genuine courage to admit to your partner when you're wrong. It takes even more courage not to attack your wife when you see a vulnerable area. It take no bravery to score an easy point when she has dropped her guard. That kind of score-keeping requires no courage and has no valor. But it also takes great courage for most of us to tell our wives what we are really feeling, to drop our own guard and be vulnerable. It doesn't really matter though who is right. It matters who is loving.

4. *Focus on growth rather than blame.* By this I mean focus on your own growth, what you can learn from the situation that is causing stress in your relationship. Focusing on where you think someone else needs to grow (i.e., to learn; to change) reflects a superior, judg-

mental attitude, and makes you come through as though you are blaming and condemning your spouse.

I have observed in marriage counseling that no real change, no actual growth can take place until both partners stop throwing verbal missiles at one another.

"You never listen to me."

"Oh yeah? Well if you'd say something worthwhile maybe I'd listen."

These assaults focus on blame. "Maybe I need to listen more and try harder to hear what you mean" is focusing on growth.

5. *Develop a "servant" attitude.* We have already made a very strong case for becoming servant-leaders. One final verse on this point is 1 Corinthians 13:5, "(Love) does not seek its own (way)." Practice seeing yourself as a servant rather than a king.

6. *Be honest—with love.* Neither honesty nor love by themselves are complete. The Bible reminds us to speak the truth in love. Unless you communicate what is going on inside of you, your wife can only guess. If she must guess what she can do to meet your needs, she may end up not meeting your needs. I advise against playing the old "If you loved me, you would know" game or the "If you don't know, I'm certainly not going to tell you" game.

7. *Be courteous.* 1 Corinthians 13 says that love is always courteous; never rude. Many of us have stopped caring about what we say or do as we did when we were dating our wives. When you must say something negative, you need to be at least as thoughtful and gentle with your wife as you would be if you were speaking to a respected lady where you work or at your church. If we love our wives, they deserve the very best treatment we can give them.

8. *Be considerate.* Be aware of little things that could

make your wife's day happier. How about remembering to call home if you must be late or picking up dirty clothes or putting the top back on the toothpaste or cleaning out the sink after you shave or any of the many things that will help her know you care about what is important to her?

9. *Be creatively affectionate.* Think of new and different ways to let her know that you are thinking about her. Try anything here from "I love you notes" in the refrigerator to sending her a special card or flowers for no particular occasion. Do whatever you can think of to keep things exciting between you. One of the most common complaints wives make about their husbands is that the husbands are only tender and affectionate when they are interested in sex. The message our wives want us to get is that they like us to be tender and affectionate at other times too.

10. *Be lovable.* Do you remember the attention you used to give your own looks and smells when you were trying to win the affections of your wife? You wanted to be as easy to love as possible. You paid great attention to details because you didn't want to give her any reason to be turned off by you. Do that again. If you won her love before, work now to keep it growing. Spend time alone together. Go out on dates. Be interested in her. Be fun to be with. It won't be as threatening this time around because you know she loves you, but keeping your love and interest fresh is just as important as winning it the first time.

Who Can Measure Up?

You may be feeling that we have been talking about some idealistic, high-sounding goals for men in this and the preceding chapters. I would have to agree with you that the scriptural standards for the loving servant-leader are far more than a code of simple dos and don'ts. When we recognize and accept our God-given assignment to serve as the heads of our homes, we can expect to have some stretching, hurting times on our way toward these ideals. But ideals are good. They show us what we are working toward and at the same time, like the Ten Commandments, they show us how we fall short of the biblical standard.

As men struggling alone and in our own strength, which one of us can fully measure up? The answer is that none of us can. We are driven to depend on the perfect servant-leader, Jesus Christ, the source of unlimited love. And that is an excellent position in which to be living.

A SELECTED BIBLIOGRAPHY FOR ADDITIONAL READING

- Ahlem, Lloyd H. *Do I Have to Be Me?* (G/L Publications, 1973). Presents a biblical basis for understanding our basic physical, emotional and spiritual needs.
- Andelin, Aubrey. *Man of Steel and Velvet* (Pacific Press, 1972). A sensible and forthright guide to what it takes to be a man and how to be one.
- Augsburger, David. *Caring Enough to Confront* (G/L Publications, 1973). Tells how to confront others when conflict arises by speaking the truth in love.
- _____. *Cherishable: Love and Marriage* (Herald, 1971). A conversation piece for couples who want to explore creative interaction in communications, finances, parenthood, values and many more.

- Biller, Henry B. *Father, Child, and Sex Role* (D.C. Heath & Co., 1971). An explanation of paternal factors in the child's sex-role development.
- Bower, Robert. *Solving Problems in Marriage* (Eerdmans, 1972). Tells how to deal with marital problems and build a strong, rewarding marriage.
- Collins, Gary, ed. *Living and Growing Together* (Word, 1976). Selected authors tell how to deepen the ties and strengthen the spiritual dimension of the home.
- —————. *Make More of Your Marriage* (Word, 1976). Selected authors offer positive and practical suggestions on how to improve your marriage.
- —————. *The Secrets of Our Sexuality* (Word, 1976). Nine authors deal frankly with the psychological, spiritual and physical dimensions of sex.
- Concordia Sex Education Series (Concordia, 1967).
  Book 1: Frey, Marguerite K. *I Wonder, I Wonder.*
  Book 2: Hummel, Ruth S. *Wonderfully Made.*
  Book 3: Bueltmann, August J. *Take the High Road.*
  Book 4: Witt, Elmer N. *Life Can Be Sexual.*
  Book 5: Kolb, Erwin J. *Parent's Guide to Christian Conversation About Sex.*
  Book 6: Wessler, Martin. *Christian View of Sex Education.*

An excellent age-graded series that offers positive help for conveying biological facts to children along with relevant Christian concepts.
- Dobson, James. *Dare to Discipline* (Tyndale, 1970). A highly recommended approach to child management that provides for disciplinary activity within the framework of love and affection.
- —————. *Hide or Seek* (Revell, 1974). Explains what actions and attitudes help to build esteem in children from infancy onward.

- _____. *What Wives Wish Their Husbands Knew About Women* (Tyndale, 1975). Reflects the vital role men play in meeting their wives' unique emotional needs and aspirations.
- Dodson, Fitzhugh. *How to Father.* A comprehensive guide to help fathers maximize their unique role on the parenting team. Has detailed appendices on toys and reading materials.
- Drakeford, John W. *Do You Hear Me, Honey?* (Harper & Row, 1976). Provides families with a primer for understanding the distortions in their communication.
- Getz, Gene A. *The Measure of a Family* (G/L Publications, 1977). Tells how God measures a family and how He sets it free to develop its own relevant family goals and standards.
- _____. *The Measure of a Man* (G/L Publications, 1974). A biblical profile for Christian maturity in a man.
- Hardisty, Margaret. *Forever My Love* (Harvest House, 1975). An explanation for husbands of the physical, emotional and psychical make-up of their wives and how to elicit their best responses.
- Haystead, Wes. *You Can't Begin Too Soon* (G/L Publications, 1974). Combines sound biblical advice and educational insights to introduce young children to Christian concepts.
- Hendricks, Howard. *Heaven Help the Home* (Scripture Press, 1973). A lively guide for parents who want to "turn out durable, functional and winsome people to represent Jesus Christ in a stormy age."
- Kilgore, James. *Being a Man in a Woman's World* (Harvest House, 1975). Tells how to be free and still face masculine responsibilities as well as how to meet the expectations of females in today's society.

- Landorf, Joyce. *Tough and Tender* (Revell, 1975). A woman's-eye view of the qualities most wives look for in their men.
- MacDonald, Gordon. *Magnificent Marriage* (Tyndale, 1976). Demonstrates that a successful marriage consists of a balance of four essential elements: romance, companionship, service and sexuality.
- Narramore, Bruce. *An Ounce of Prevention* (Zondervan, 1973). Suggests a sound, purposeful plan for guiding children's moral development and internalizing values.
- _____. *Help, I'm a Parent* (Zondervan, 1973). An inviting guide to parenthood that establishes a solid basis for rearing children by drawing on both biblical and psychological truth.
- Narramore, Clyde. *How to Succeed in Family Living* (G/L Publications, 1968). Establishes biblical standards against which husband and wife, parents and children can measure their conduct and interaction.
- Osborne, Cecil. *The Art of Understanding Your Mate* (Zondervan, 1970). A realistic approach to marriage born out of the author's many hours of counseling married couples whose relationships were in trouble.
- Petersen, J. Allan, ed. *For Men Only* (Tyndale, 1973). An array of experienced authors bring into focus the various areas of a man's world and the need for strong, confident masculine leadership in the home and the community.
- _____. *The Marriage Affair* (Tyndale, 1971). Capable contributors offer a smorgasbord of information and inspiration dealing with every phase of marriage and the family.
- _____. *Two Become One* (Tyndale, 1973). A series of 13 Bible studies on the subject of marriage and the family.

- Richards, Lawrence O. *You, the Parent* (Moody, 1974). Gives practical guiding principles to adhere to in order to be an effective parent.
- Rickerson, Wayne. *Good Times for Your Family* (G/L Publications, 1976). A collection of over 100 family fun ideas which build communication and teach Christian values and Bible truths.
- Scanzoni, Letha. *Sex Is a Parent Affair* (G/L Publications, 1973). An excellent book for parents who want to guide their children toward a responsible understanding of a realistic, biblical plan for sex.
- Shedd, Charlie W. *Letters to Philip* (Word, 1970). A frank look at the male role—the dos and taboos of dealing with women.
- _____. *Smart Dads I Know* (Sheed and Ward, Inc., 1975). Reveals problems many families have and how certain fathers provided their own unique solutions for their own family situations.
- _____. *You Can Be a Great Parent!* (Word, 1970). The author gives his own successful plan for family living along with sensible and specific solutions for all kinds of everyday crises in child-rearing.
- Small, Dwight H. *After You've Said I Do* (Revell, 1968). How to deal with the inevitable questions, problems and disagreements after the honeymoon is over.
- _____. *Christian, Celebrate Your Sexuality!* (Revell, 1974). Offers the mature Christian a larger, freer and more fulfilling view of what it means to be male and female.
- Temple, Joe. *Know Your Child* (Baker Books, 1974). Stresses in clear, "how-to" language the ways to guide a child in the direction of his own God-given capabilities.
- Tournier, Paul. *To Understand Each Other* Trans. by

John S. Gilmour (John Knox, 1967). Suggests ways for couples to achieve real understanding and work out marital happiness together.

- Trobisch, Walter. *I Married You* (Harper & Row, 1971). A unique portrayal through narratives of the joys and problems inherent in the marriage partnership.
- Vincent, Maurice O. *God, Sex and You* (Lippincott, 1971). A survey of sex, society and God from the Old Testament to the new morality.
- Wagner, Maurice. *The Sensation of Being Somebody* (Zondervan, 1975). Enables the reader to clearly discern the personal factors that have shaped his self-concept so that he can build emotional security and an adequate self-concept.
- Wakefield, Norm. *You Can Have a Happier Family* (G/L Publications, 1977). Shares warm and practical guidelines based on biblical principles for developing a Christian family life-style.
- Williams, H. Page. *Do Yourself a Favor: Love Your Wife* (Logos International, 1973). A manual for men who want to become what God intended and make their marriages come alive.
- Wright, H. Norman. *An Answer to Discipline* (Harvest House, 1976). Offers brief and practical advice on effective methods of discipline, establishing rules which bring about change, and getting children to talk and listen, among others.
- _____. *Communication: Key to Your Marriage* (G/L Publications, 1974). Discusses ways to communicate at new and deeper levels, to understand your mate better and to cope with marital conflict.